YEAR OF THE MONKEY

By

Gene Hays

1st Printing April 2010

For Lynda, Margo and Barbara

The poet was in love
He went to the mountain to begin his climb
There he met an angel
And the angel said to the poet,
What can you do without that you can't do without
within?

The poet replied,
Well, without …I can do without everything
I can even do without me
But within, I need love
And the angel smiled and sent the poet to the stars,
The planets and the heavens
Because he knew that love is forever.

Richard F. Risner
Sunrise - February 23, 1932
Sunset - January 27, 2005
Beloved Husband, Father, Grandfather,
Friend and Marine
Hero

Summer 1955, Somewhere in the East China Sea

The behemoth rose from the depths of the ocean floor like a giant whale displacing water all around it. The noise the submarine made by surfacing was quickly lost in the choppy waves. A lone figure emerged from the vessel climbing up to the conning tower. The Naval officer produced a pair of binoculars and began to search in a 360 degree circle. The moon was eclipsed but visibility was good thanks to the almost cloudless sky dotted with millions of stars. The officer stopped panning to the starboard side of the ship when he detected a small group of lights coming from an island in the distance. It was an island named Diaoyu. He picked up a microphone and spoke a few barely audible words to the crew below. Almost instantly one figure after another climbed through the open hatch and onto the deck until four men were assembled on the fore deck of the sub. Three of the men wore wet suits and one was dressed in blue dungarees. The three in wet suits wore 45 caliber pistols and K-Bar knives attached to cartridge belts around their waists. All were of equal height but the leader looked like a body builder, his muscles bulging through his wet suit. He was Marine Second Lieutenant Richard F. Risner, United States Marine Corps Reserve. The other two Marines in wetsuits were named Private First Class Richard M. Petterson and buck Private Charley Redfeather. Wordlessly the three men untied a rubber raft attached to the deck of the sub while the sailor in dungarees began retrieving oars and additional weapons from the crew below. The Lieutenant and the Private First Class were handed Thompson 45 caliber grease guns and the Private was given a Browning automatic rifle. They slung them over their shoulders.

Continuing in silence the three climbed into the rubber raft and waited until the deck was clear and then they cast off as the submarine began to submerge. Redfeather began to paddle in the direction of the lights. The raft approached from the east side of the island concealed by the trees and surrounding vegetation. The sound of waves breaking across the coral reefs and rock foundations muffled any sound of the raft landing on the beach. Petterson and Redfeather quickly and silently lowered themselves into the water and pulled the raft to shore. Redfeather assumed a defensive position on the beach with his BAR at the ready. The other two moved slowly and cautiously in the direction of the lights constantly surveying the area around them.

Coming to a clearing, they quickly dropped to their knees and assumed the prone position at the bank of a rice paddy. Risner raised a pair of binoculars to his eyes to ensure that no one was observing them from the rice paddy. Confident they wouldn't be seen; the two men rose to a crouched position and with Risner in front, slowly and noiselessly entered the rice paddy. With only the tops of their torsos exposed, they moved slowly with their pistols held above the rice paddy. Reaching the other side and only 20 meters from the edge of the compound, Risner climbed out of the rice paddy on his stomach with Petterson following. They continued to crawl for the next few minutes listening for any sounds or movement around them. The camp was quiet, almost surreal. Reaching a thicket that provided cover, both Marines stopped and took a careful survey of their surroundings. Looking in the direction from where they came, they did not hear or see anyone except for the muted sounds of the ocean waves lapping at the beach. To their right and left, they could see an almost natural barrier around the camp. The inside had been cleverly cleared of any ground vegetation but the overgrowth at tree-top level provided a natural cover from the sky. It would have been nearly impossible to see the camp from the air or sea. The outside perimeter looked to be about 100 meters on the long sides and about half that on the ends. There were no fences or other barriers around the perimeter.

Looking across the camp, the two Marines could see guard towers at two corners of the camp. They were nearest the corner tower to their right, but they could clearly see the cross-corner tower to the other side even without moonlight. Adjusting their vision to the only two light sources in front of them, both towers appeared to be unmanned. Petterson made a hand sign as if to ask "where are the guards?" Risner only shrugged his shoulders and moved his head from side to side showing he didn't see anything either. Concentrating on the main building in the right front corner of the camp they were able to see a soft glow of light through a partially covered window of a Quonset hut that was the command center. The hut was about 15 meters square with a half-round tin roof over it. A cable ran between the hut and a nearby antenna tower about 20 meters tall concealed by foliage. A 10 meter flag pole with a Red Chinese flag attached waved briefly with small changes in the wind. Listening carefully, they could hear the faint sounds of an Asian radio station playing oriental music. No one was in sight anywhere in the compound. The only other source of light was another Quonset hut to their left that appeared to be the quarters area. A soft light from another window suggested that someone was there. With no visible evidence of guards or any human presence, Risner moved to his side placing his mouth at the other Marine's left ear. Whispering,

"This doesn't seem right. I want to move around the perimeter towards the other building. Keep your eyes and ears open as we move. When we get to the other side, we will be able to see our target's hut in full view across the compound as well as the rest of the camp. Our Intelligence is that there is at least one guard on our target always. Maybe he's taking a break or is inside. Let's check it out. You take the point."

Nodding his agreement, Petterson moved out to the right around the compound. As they made their way around there was no other sign of activity. Vents coming up from the ground at various intervals around the compound suggested that there were underground rooms or tunnels. Reaching the first corner they saw from the ground that the tower directly above them was empty. As they approached the far corner, they still could not hear anything other than the radio that was playing music. The Lieutenant signaled the other Marine to stay in place while he moved along side the building. Staying below the window level he poked his head slightly above the window. He immediately saw that the source of light was coming from an underground room not a desk lamp in the office. He could see the stairs leading down from the middle of the room to below. He could also see a vacuum tube radio with a lighted dial. He could not see or hear anything but assumed there had to be something going on below. Making his way back to Petterson he told him what he saw.

Then he heard a male voice from inside the building. The source of the voice seemed to be angry and was yelling. At the same time, they could hear a door open on the side opposite from them and footsteps coming towards them. Without saying anything to the other, both Marines holstered their pistols and drew their K-Bar knives silently from their sheaths. Keeping low and out of sight, they saw a figure come around the building heading towards the dense jungle perimeter only 10 meters away. He looked like a young Red Chinese soldier, the red stars displayed prominently on the shoulder straps of his tunic and a large red star on the front of his cap. If the soldier looked to his left it was doubtful that he would see the two Marines, but they were crouched and ready to pounce on him if he did. The soldier's rifle was slung over his left shoulder and he was smoking a cigarette with his right hand. Reaching the perimeter, he put the cigarette in his mouth, unzipped his fly and began to urinate. He looked briefly to his left and right and seemed to be satisfied that he was not being observed. Finishing, the soldier zipped up his fly, tossed his cigarette in the direction of the Marines and began to make his way across the compound to the other side. Once he was out of earshot the two Marines sheathed their K-Bars.

"There's our guard" Risner whispered. "He must have been sleeping somewhere in the office and I didn't see him. Check out the inside and make sure there is no one else inside before we leave."

Nodding acknowledgement, Petterson quietly moved towards the window making sure he was out of sight if the guard turned around, or if he came back to the building. He was halfway to the window when he froze in his tracks. He heard someone inside changing the radio station. He waited another couple of minutes before moving again. Shielded by the building from sight of the other guard and reaching the window, he inched upward just in time to hear the footsteps of someone descending the stairs. His first reaction was to duck down until he realized the soldier was out of view. Satisfied no one else was in the office he chanced peering intently through the window at all different angles. Making his way back to Risner he shook his head sideways showing he saw no other presence. Risner decided to continue around the perimeter in a counter-clockwise direction.

Moving silently from their hidden position, they cleared the corner of the building and saw the guard enter the target's hut. Risner signaled with his hand that he would keep an eye on the tower ahead while Petterson kept his eye on the other hut. They continued moving silently and were close to the other tower when they heard the noise of the target hut's door open. The same guard who had entered not five minutes before was now headed back to the office hut. Both Marines froze in their positions until the guard reached the office and closed the door behind him. They immediately moved to the base of the other tower where found an unmanned post.   Risner whispered:

"I don't like it. Not much security."

"I don't either," Petterson said.

"I'm also concerned now that our man might be underground instead of being in that hut.   Our Intelligence didn't say anything about underground rooms or tunnels."

"What do we do?" Petterson asked.

"We follow our orders and find our man and get him out of here."   Neither man said anything for a couple of minutes lost in their own thoughts. Looking at his military green watch, Risner continued: "We don't have a lot of time. We have to find him wherever that leads us. You know what we have to do. I'm telling you right now, I won't be taken prisoner."

Me either." Extending his right hand in a fist towards the Lieutenant they touched fists.   "Recon" they whispered together.

Both Marines moved slowly around the side of the hut stopping at the door entrance. There was no sound coming from the hut and they could not see the guard across the compound, and they hoped he wouldn't see them. They both drew their pistols silently holding them in their right hands while drawing their K-Bar knives with the left. Risner slowly opened the door as quietly as possible. As they entered the hut, there was a small quantity of light coming from a stairwell to their right that descended into the ground. There was no noise coming from anywhere. Stopping and adjusting their eyes to the light, they could see a form on a bunk, wrapped in a sleeping bag against the far wall. Looking around the room they realized something was wrong. The interior of the hut looked to be a basic apartment with a cooking space, small dining table and a section with a worn sofa and chair. There was no evidence of a guard and no evidence that the sleeping form was restrained in any way. With Petterson covering the door and watching the stairwell Risner moved towards the sleeping figure. About halfway to the bed, a board creaked loudly and the figure half rose from the bed.

"What the hell...?" the figure said reaching for a table lamp beside him and turning it on. He rubbed his eyes and asked "Who are you guys?"

Putting a finger to his lips suggesting that they whisper, Risner said softly "John, it's me, Rich."

"Rich?" He struggled to adjust his vision. "What in hell's name are you doing here? What's going on?"

"We're here to take you back, John. Come on, we need to get you out of here quickly."

"Okay, Rich, but hold on, how are we going to get out of here?"

"I don't have time to explain" Risner said.

"We've got a sub waiting on us."

Rising from the bed clad only in his underwear and rubbing his eyes, John said, "Okay, let me get my clothes on."

"Hurry" Risner said.

As John made his way to a makeshift wooden closet, he opened the door and reached in for his clothes. When his hand came out he was holding a 45 caliber pistol. Risner heard Petterson's pistol go off behind him, a split second before he fired. Both Marines watched as the target fell to the floor killed instantly from 2 bullets straight through the heart. It all happened so quickly that John never had a chance to fire his weapon. Risner was temporarily dumbfounded. He had reacted as he had been trained but he couldn't believe what had just happened.

At precisely the same moment that the shots were fired, a Red Chinese Officer's head appeared from the stairwell to Risner's left, holding a bottle of beer in one hand and a bowl of rice in the other. Separated from Risner by less than 5 meters with only his upper torso exposed, he stared stupidly at Risner's face for what seemed an eternity but was only a few seconds. By the time Risner wheeled to his left and shot at his adversary, the officer had dropped both the bottle and plate and dove for cover. The errant shot went over his head.

"Lieutenant Risner, we have to get out of here, now!" Petterson said.

Risner could only nod his head agreeing. Both Marines bolted out the door and made for the rice paddy. Within 30 seconds of the first shots being fired the camp suddenly came to life. By this time the two Marines had reached the perimeter and spotlights illuminated the entire compound in the towers. Voices were yelling all around the compound and Red Chinese soldiers burst from the two buildings carrying weapons. As the Marines reached the rice paddy they split in two directions. They ran on both sides of the rice paddy not able to see the 10 soldiers pursuing them. As planned, Private Redfeather had moved up to the rice paddy and set-up his Browning Automatic Rifle with a tripod mount. As Risner was rounding the corner of the rice paddy he saw that Petterson had been a little faster and would reach Redfeather before he did. At the same time, the Private opened with short bursts from the automatic rifle slowing the advance of the Red Chinese killing four of them at once. The enemy soldiers dropped to protective cover and zeroed in on Redfeather. Unknown to the others, Redfeather was wounded when a round found his shoulder but he continued to fire without pause. Moving quickly the two Marines made their way past Redfeather towards the beach. Both of them knew that they could not offer any help with their pistols. They made their way to the raft where they got their Thompson sub-machine guns and waited for Redfeather, ready to provide covering fire if needed. Redfeather kept the soldiers at bay, keeping his fire bursts short so as not to overheat the barrel of his automatic rifle.

The next two minutes seemed like hours to the two Marines on the beach as they wanted to rush to the aid of their comrade but they needed to protect their position. Waiting until he was sure that Risner and Petterson were back at the raft, Redfeather left his position and ran towards his two comrades. Small arms fire continued for a few seconds and then stopped completely. As Redfeather reached the front of the raft, automatic rifle in hand, the other two Marines were in the water knee deep, ready to get back in the raft and paddle out to sea. Redfeather bent over, dumped the automatic rifle into the raft and began to push the raft with the other two Marines covering him. Suddenly three Red Chinese soldiers appeared from the right flank firing their weapons towards the three Marines. Petterson was the first to be hit in his shoulder and then as Redfeather turned he took a gut shot. Risner fired his Thompson at the soldier who had shot Petterson, killing the Chinese soldier instantly, nearly decapitating him. Turning his weapon towards the soldier who had shot Redfeather, he fired a short burst into the soldier's chest. Petterson killed the third Chinese soldier with a head shot between the eyes. The soldier who had shot Redfeather was mortally wounded by Risner. Using his last ounce of strength the enemy soldier dropped his rifle and pulled a grenade from his jacket as he was going down. No one saw the grenade except for Redfeather. As the grenade rolled towards the three Marines, Redfeather shouted:

"Grenade!" and covered it with his body. His now lifeless body absorbed the full impact of the grenade. Risner helped the wounded Petterson crawl over and into the raft. Not about to leave one of his men behind, Risner quickly picked Redfeather up and placed him in the raft. Propelling the raft out to sea, Risner and Petterson who had the use of only one arm paddled back towards the submarine. Redfeather had saved them both, making the ultimate sacrifice. No one spoke until they reached the side of the submarine. Petterson said to Risner: "You know we were set-up," making it more of a statement than a question. Risner only nodded his head in agreement.

August 1967, Da Nang, Republic of South Vietnam

Major Richard F. Risner, United States Marine Corps Reserve, stood over 6 feet tall and weighed around 220 pounds and did not have an ounce of fat on his body. His military pedigree was as follows: he was born in Chicago, Illinois in 1932. He attended high school in Sioux City, Iowa and received his Bachelor of Science degree from Augustana College in Sioux Falls, South Dakota. He received his commission as a 2nd Lieutenant, United States Marine Corps Reserve, from Officer Candidate School in Quantico, Virginia in 1955. He served tours of duty in Korea and Japan with the 3rd Marine Division Rear in 1955 and 1956. During this time Lieutenant Risner was the Platoon Leader of Private First Class Dick Petterson. On promotion to 1st Lieutenant and his return to the States, Risner became Commanding Officer of "C" Company, 1st Battalion, 5th Marines at Camp Pendleton, California. From 1959 to 1965, Risner served as Executive Officer and then on promotion to Captain, became the Commanding Officer of the 27th Infantry Company, United States Marine Corps Reserve, in Sioux City, Iowa. During this time he taught school and coached football and track at West Junior High School in Sioux City. He received his Master of Arts degree from the University of South Dakota in 1964. On completion of his MA, Risner was promoted to Major and transferred to active duty in 1965 and was assigned as the Commanding Officer, Schools

15

Company, Schools Battalion, Marine Corps Base Camp Pendleton, California. In August of 1967, Major Risner was ordered to report to the Commanding General, Third Marine Amphibious Force in DaNang, Republic of South Vietnam.

Normally when ordered to report to a Commanding General one begins by going to headquarters and to the personnel officer who could be anything from a Captain to a Lieutenant Colonel. If the assignment was pre-ordained, one would be given a check-in sheet and begin to make the rounds for billeting assignment and all the other various stops needed to get settled in. This could last for three to five days culminating in the last stop of the check-in process: your ultimate place of work assignment. Major Risner was directed to report to the Commanding General in person. Normally only the very senior Officers would report directly to the General when they first checked in. Major General Lewis Walt was the overall Commander of all Marine Forces, Air and Ground in the northern most area of South Vietnam known as I (eye) Corps. Four other Corps areas, II through V to the south of I Corps, were commanded by Army Generals. Overall Commander was General William C. Westmoreland, United States Army, Commander of Military Assistance Command Vietnam. General Walt had two bosses: operationally he reported to General Westmoreland; administratively he reported to Lieutenant General Victor (Brute) Krulak, Commanding General of Fleet Marine Forces Pacific.

"Major Richard F. Risner reporting as ordered,

Sir!" He barked as he marched within 3 paces of the front of the desk of General Walt and braced himself at attention. From a sitting position, Walt replied:

"At ease, Major. Pull up a chair and light one if you have it-unless you care for one of these Havanas," pointing to the humidor on the corner of his desk. "You know, we can't buy these in the States but I've got a good friend who gets them from Vice President Ky in Saigon."

"No thank you Sir, with the General's permission I'll go ahead and light up a Pall Mall." Walt nodded and Risner sat in one of the chairs to Walt's right.

"Rich" he began "you do go by Rich don't you?" and he didn't wait for him to respond. "I know you are wondering why you were sent to me first and I want you to know that I have a very important assignment for you."

"I'm honored Sir, but I don't know what I have done to merit anything special."

"Save the humility speech Major. General Krulak told me what you did in Korea."

Risner looked surprise. Walt explained, "I know it was a covert operation but Krulak thought I should know something about your background. I know you have an outstanding record save for a brush with one of your senior officers at the Officer's Club at Pendleton." He smiled as Risner visibly blushed in embarrassment recalling in his mind how as a Captain he had punched out the running lights of another Captain who was senior to him. Walt continued:

"From what I understand, he had it coming."

Somewhat nonplussed Risner replied, "He shouldn't have made disparaging remarks about my mother, Sir. She was definitely married to my father when I was born."

At that, Walt laughed out loud. Turning serious Walt leaned forward in his chair. "Rich, we have a problem with the combat strategy of the Army. General Westmoreland has decided that we will wage a war of attrition with the North Vietnamese. He wants us to hunt them down in as large a number as we can find at one time. The problem with that strategy is the requirement to have good Intelligence so we know where to find them since they are constantly on the move. We can engage them on a hill on one day, own the hill the next and then have to leave it to go find the enemy again. When we move out they re-take the same hill. They threaten and murder the Village Chiefs and Elders and their families if they help us and tell the villagers they will be back when we leave. We are paying the price for the same piece of ground repeatedly and the enemy simply sends more troops in from the North. With the emphasis from Military Assistance Command Vietnam on body counts and prisoners of war taken, I can tell from the reporting of the other four Corps areas that the numbers are being inflated just to please the command. The numbers being reported for the prisoners of war captured don't reflect the fact that most of the prisoners of war are being released after 3-5 days if the Army of the Republic of Vietnam doesn't pick them up and transfer them to Saigon."

As Risner began to speak, Walt cut him off: "I know you are wondering why I'm telling you all this but bear with me. Both General Krulak and I believe the key to win this war is to win the hearts and minds of the locals with the result of denying sanctuary to the enemy. The North Vietnamese Army and Viet Cong can only survive with support from the locals. If we embed Marines in the local villages and hamlets we can use a three-prong strategy where first, our Marines can learn some of the language and customs; we engender support and root out the Viet Cong using the County Fair strategy. That means gathering all the locals and systematically identifying the good guys from the bad. We issue identification cards to the good and kill the bad. The second prong of equal importance is training the Popular Forces to use weapons and to provide for their own defense. There is no way we can win this war if the Popular Forces and local leaders can't defend themselves. The third prong is performing Civic Action projects where we use our Navy Corpsmen and Doctors to treat the villagers and we provide materials for building and repairing schools and other infrastructure. Have you heard of Lieutenant Colonel William Corson?"

Risner replied, "I have heard his name in conjunction with the Combined Action Platoons."

"That's him. Corson is the Commanding Officer of all the Combined Action Groups, Companies and Platoons. Shortly after our arrival in force in 1965, we started the Combined Action Platoons or CAPs. Each unit consists of a fifteen-man rifle squad assigned to a particular hamlet in the Marine tactical area of responsibility. CAP units work with platoons of local Vietnamese militia. CAP Marines are volunteers with combat experience who are given basic instruction on Vietnamese culture and customs. These combined units conduct night patrols and ambushes, gradually making the local Vietnamese forces assume a greater share of responsibility for village security. Their mission is the destruction of the National Liberation Front/Viet Cong infrastructure, organization of local intelligence networks, and the military training of the Popular Forces. By January of 1966 we had 7 CAP units and we now have 57."

Pausing for a moment as if to collect his thoughts, Walt went to his humidor and took one of the Havanas in his left hand and rolled it between his fingers. Next he held the cigar beneath his nose and savored the aroma. Reaching back to the humidor with his right hand he pulled out a cigar cutter, clipped the end, disposed of the clipping and returned the cutter to the humidor. He then picked up a Zippo lighter embossed with a Marine Corps Eagle, Globe and Anchor emblem and lit the cigar. "You don't mind do you?" and without waiting for a reply he continued.

"I'm hoping that the number of CAP units will double by the end of next year. When we started we all understood that the war in Vietnam could not be won solely by defeating large units of the enemy. Attention to counterinsurgency operations would be necessary to remove the political influence of the National

Liberation Front, particularly in the rural areas of South Vietnam."

The National Front for the Liberation of South Vietnam consisted of a political arm of the Communist Party in North Vietnam and a military arm in the Viet Cong in South Vietnam. Walt continued: "Westmoreland is convinced that the emphasis should remain focused on conventional warfare and the interdiction of the enemy's external support mechanisms. He thinks large unit operations are the key to victory, and small unit operations should be largely ignored. On the other hand, we have adopted a strategic approach that emphasizes pacification over large-unit battles. Hell, even McNamara back in 1962 on a tour with General Krulak said the key to winning is getting the PFs trained and equipped to defend the small villages and hamlets. Now it seems they both think that will take too long."

General Walt stood up from behind his desk and as he did he motioned with his hand for Major Risner to stay seated. He pointed to his left to 2 maps on the wall. One map was labeled at the top "1965" and the other labeled "Present." Both were maps of the I Corps area with red colored push pins designating enemy held areas and blue colored push pins designating pacified areas containing CAP units. The "1965" map had at least 10 times the red pins for every blue pin. The "Present" map was just the opposite. "Rich, I think you can see that this program has succeeded far beyond our most optimistic hopes. In slightly more than two years after the initiation of CAP units, a US

Department of Defense report shows that the Hamlet Evaluation System security score gave CAP-protected villages a score of 2.95 out of a possible 5.0 maximum, compared with an average of 1.6 for all I Corps villages. There is a direct correlation between the time a CAP stays in a village and the degree of security achieved, with CAP-protected villages progressing twice as fast as those occupied by the Popular Forces militia alone. The casualty rates for CAP units are lower than that of units conducting search-and-destroy missions. One of our British allies is a counterinsurgency expert named General Richard Clutterbuck. He has noted that although Marine casualties are high, they are only fifty percent of the casualties of the normal infantry battalions being maneuvered by helicopters on large scale operations. The extension rate of Marines serving in CAP units is exceeding sixty percent, and there are no recorded desertions of Popular Force soldiers from CAP units. The Viet Cong have never regained control of a hamlet protected by one of our CAP units."

Walt held his hands up in a sign suggesting that he didn't understand as he regained his seat behind his desk. "And would you believe our Commander, General Westmoreland, has actually complained to the Army Chief of Staff and the Secretary of Defense that our Marines seem to be complacent staying in the villages and that they are reluctant to leave and pursue the enemy?" Shaking his head in disbelief, Walt continued,

"Last summer, General Krulak even went so far as to go

over Westmoreland's head to McNamara and asked for an audience with the President. When President Johnson received him, Krulak explained his strategy for winning the war which included Pacification and strategic bombing of North Vietnam. At this point, the President took Krulak by the arm and explained he had already decided on Westmoreland's plan of engaging large numbers of the enemy and showed him the door."

Walt puffed on his cigar with an obvious look of disdain on his face as he weighed what he would say next. "The problem is that Krulak has 3 stars to Westmoreland's 4. So Westmoreland has agreed to let me continue with the CAP program but the numbers have to come out of our Table of Organization staffing. In other words, 1 Marine out of every 10 is being assigned to a CAP unit. That means my operational combat units are operating at 90% of their staffing. I struggle with these numbers every day as I look at the casualty reports. The numbers show that even though we are operating below optimum manning level in the large operational engagements we are suffering smaller numbers of casualties as compared with the Army. We are not sacrificing Marine lives to prove that a strategy is flawed but just the opposite."

Pointing again to the "Present" map he continued, "The map proves my point Rich. And the intelligence shows that the North Vietnamese Army is now moving into the southern part of I Corps and below." Turning his gaze back to Major Risner he said, "This is where you come into play, Major. I am sending you to Chu Lai." Anticipating Risner's lack of understanding he continued, "I know there are no major Marine infantry units there. We have the air field with two aircraft groups and supporting units in the 9th Engineer Battalion as well as a Combined Action Group and CAP units. The Army's Americal Division has the overall responsibility for the defense of that area but I have overall control over the air field and our Marine Aviation units through Colonel Bill White the Commanding Officer of the Air Base. You will be assigned to Marine Aircraft Group 12 administratively as the Ground Defense Officer but operationally you will come under the Americal Division Ground Defense Officer. It is paramount that we protect the A-6 Intruder Aircraft based there as well as the F-4 Phantoms, A-4 Skyhawks and EA6A Prowlers. That means you will be responsible for the defense of Sub-Sector 4 of the Chu Lai Defense command-that's the entire air base and all of the Marine Corps, Army and Air Force aviation units located there. We are concerned about the upcoming TET celebration in January of 1968 and that brings me to your secondary duty. I am assigning you a collateral duty as the Civic Action Officer for Marine Aircraft Group 12. I have arranged for you to meet with Lieutenant Colonel Corson tomorrow for a briefing. In short, you won't have any problems with Bill White or the individual Commanding Officers; they know you are coming. The Army however may be a different story. You will come under Lieutenant Colonel Warren Lucas who is the Provost Marshall and Officer in Charge of Chu Lai Defense Command. In any event, you take any problems you can't resolve to Lieutenant Colonel R.C. Barton."

He paused for another moment as he flicked off the growing ash on the end of his cigar into an ashtray. He leaned forward as if he were going to whisper. "Bob is an Academy Marine as am I. He is presently the Executive Officer and he knows you are coming. He reports to Colonel Dan Alexander who is the Commanding Officer of the group. Dan is a Naval Aviator who spends most of his time trying to earn as many air medals as he can. He doesn't know that Bob Barton reports to me directly. So after you leave this office there will be no further direct communication between us unless I initiate it. You go through Bob and he'll get to me; understood?"

"Yes Sir, I do."

"Good. You should also know that Bob is very close to one of the Vietnamese concession owners. Her name is Madame Huyen. She and her partner, Madame Ba live aboard the Marine Aircraft Group 12 compound where the Marine Exchange Store and concession area is." Leaning back into his chair he continued: "That's a violation of a Military Assistance Command Vietnam order that states that no indigenous personnel will remain aboard any U.S. compound overnight." Smiling he said, "At first it was allowed because the ladies feared reprisals from the North Vietnamese Army and Viet Cong so they were kept aboard for their security. Now they continue to live there. Madame Huyen is the sister of a friend of mine named Madame Hai. Madame Hai used to own this rock quarry we sit on right now called Da Nang. We couldn't pay her for it but we lease it from her by giving her all of the concession rights throughout Vietnam. That has made her a millionaire and she is good friends with all of the American leaders, military and otherwise."

Leaning forward again he said: "Bob is close to her because she gives us good intelligence from sources both for and against us. It does not hurt that she is a lovely and charming woman so Bob keeps her happy."

Rising from his chair made Major Risner stand up at attention. Walt grabbed his cover and said: "Follow me outside Major."

Leaving the General's office, Walt headed out through the front door with Risner following, causing everyone to come to attention as he strolled past their desks and outside into the bright sunlight. The General turned to the right and headed towards some wooden steps that descended into the ground with sandbags over and around the opening. A Marine with a Military Police armband, armed with a 45 caliber pistol swiftly came to attention and saluted. Walt and Risner returned the salute as they went down the stairs into a small cavern brightly lit with field radios and maps on desks and smaller tunnels leading off in three different directions. There were rifles, machine guns, grenades and 3.5 inch rocket launchers stored strategically around the cavern. There were four other Marines on duty talking on the field radios with one Marine wearing a headset operating a small switchboard. Risner heard him as he plugged in one of the connectors and announced: "Third MAF Headquarters, can I help you, Sir?" No one looked up to see the General as they went about their jobs.

"This is my Command Center, Major Risner," he explained. "You will also have a smaller version in Chu Lai. When we come under attack this is where we plan our defensive and/or offensive strategy. I have communications set up between all air and ground units as well as tactical communications with every Major command in I Corps. That includes lines to the Army, Navy, Air Force and Military Assistance Command Vietnam Headquarters in Saigon." He paused to let that sink in.

"The real reason I am sending you to Chu Lai, Rich is that we have pretty good intelligence that the North Vietnamese Army is trying to cut us off from Chu Lai. That would enable them to disrupt our air campaigns in the De-Militarized Zone and the north and make both Da Nang and Chu Lai more vulnerable to a ground attack. We figure this will happen in conjunction with the TET observance of 1968. Our intelligence reports indicate that men and supplies are being moved from North Vietnam to South Vietnam by use of the Ho Chi Minh trail. They will use this time to take control of as many villages and hamlets as they can and store food and munitions to bolster their effort when they are ready to attack. We do not have enough CAP units to keep all of the enemy forces from accomplishing this mission so it's important that we get a Pacification program in place, working and expanding, between now and next January. Walking over to one of the maps on the wall that was labeled

Chu Lai, Walt pointed at the red push pins. "The reds indicate enemy held areas, the blues are clear of the enemy and the yellows are friendly by day, enemy by night. As you can see, Major, the blues and the yellows are around 20-25% of the total. It would be generous to say they make up 30%. We need to reverse those numbers and get at least 80 to 90 percent control or we put all of I Corps at risk. We know from the reports of our units in Northern I Corps that the enemy is concentrating further South and I want to get them to bypass I Corps all together and head into the Mekong Delta region where it will be more difficult for them to operate. It was also put them in a 'kill zone' where we have our Army and South Vietnamese forces waiting for them."

Walt turned in the direction of the center tunnel motioning for Risner to follow him. The tunnel was 8 feet tall and 6 feet across. Light bulbs hung from the ceiling about every 20 feet. They had gone no more than 10 feet when they came to a wooden door on the right. It was simply labeled with 2 stars. Just as the General reached for the handle to open the door, the light bulbs throughout the Command Bunker flickered on and off and the muted sounds of sirens wailing could be faintly heard throughout the bunker.

"Incoming" Walt announced. "Sounds like Charley is giving you a welcome aboard," the General chuckled slightly. "Come on in Major and close the door behind you."

The General's office was a room about 15 feet square with a military style folding field table in the middle and four metal chairs positioned in front of and to the sides of the desk. The chair behind the desk was a wooden high-back chair with a cushioned seat. A field phone was placed on one corner of the desk and a desk blotter covered most of the top of the desk. A large map of I Corps similar to the one in his main office was attached to the wall behind the General's chair. The map was covered with a thin layer of plastic and that was colored over with multi-color markers. Throughout the bunker the sides and ceiling were reinforced with wood planking and the floor was dirt. "Have a chair Major" Walt said as he sat in the chair behind his desk. About that same time a slight vibration rocked the room with the muted sound of a "crack!" Fine particles of dust floated from the ceiling.

"That's unusual," Walt quipped. "That was undoubtedly a B-40 rocket that landed fairly close. They don't usually hit us during the daylight hours."

The field phone on Walt's desk came alive with a ringing sound. Picking up the phone the General said "Walt here."

The General listened for about a minute without saying anything then said, "Keep me posted, Captain." Looking at Major Risner he explained. "That last rocket hit pretty close but one of our spotters in the tower thinks he's got a location on the launcher. They'll send in a Huey gunship to take it out if Charley is still there. He was definitely a good shot" Walt said smiling. "He took out one of our shitters and scared the hell out of a Lieutenant who was just finishing."

The phone rang again and Walt picked it up

without speaking. "Thank you Captain" he said placing the phone back in its cradle. "That was the all clear. Charley's finished for now. Back to your mission, Major. When you meet with Corson tomorrow you've got all day to pick his brain and get a sense of what he is doing and what he has accomplished. After that I want you to get down to Chu Lai and start working. Your position down there is brand new so you will be writing your own Standard Operating Procedures. Your main purpose Rich is to work your Tactical Area of Responsibility as thoroughly and as quickly as you can to get as many of those villages and hamlets colored blue."

Risner asked "What is my Tactical Area of Responsibility, General?"

"It will be up to you as to how far you can effectively cover the area. Ideally, I would like you to covering an area 20 kilometers north to Tam Ky from Chu Lai and 35 kilometers south to Quang Ngai. Of course your border on the east is the ocean and your border on the west is the mountains separating you from Laos."

Risner looked surprised and then asked, "Doesn't the Army have responsibility for some of that area?"

"Yes and so does Marine Aircraft Group 13, 9th Engineers, the Navy Seabees and some of our CAP units. Your authority trumps any of theirs. Once again if that causes problems you need to resolve them yourself or go to Bob Barton. Find out what they are doing and why they are failing to pacify that area.

Identify and rectify the situation Major."

"Aye, aye Sir" Risner replied. "What about my staff?"

"You will be the Staff, Major. Hand-pick you a Staff Non-Commissioned Officer to be your Non-Commissioned Officer in Charge and four other enlisted men. I am assigning you a Vietnamese Marine Interpreter who will be supplied by the Vietnamese Army Command in Saigon. I have asked Personnel to provide you with a list of in-country Marines who have been through Defense Language Institute in Monterey California for the Vietnamese short course of 3 months. General Krulak wisely made the decision to send 10% of all troops inbound to Vietnam to be trained in the Vietnamese language regardless of their occupational specialty. Barton will make sure you get whoever you want."

Risner replied "I already know who I want for the Staff Non-Commissioned Officer but I don't know where he is."

Walt reached for his field phone and cranked the wheel twice. "Get me Personnel please." After a few moments "Major Toner this is General Walt. I'm sending Major Rich Risner to you later today. He's going to give you the name of a Staff Non-Commissioned Officer that he wants to be a part of his team. See if you can find him." Walt listened for a minute.

"If he's in-country get him to Marine Aircraft Group 12 in Chu Lai. If he's in the Continental United States message the Commandant of the Marine Corps that we want him transferred here ASAP. Make the request on behalf of General Krulak and myself." He paused again. "Thank you Major."

He placed the phone back in its cradle. "Last but not least, one very important part of your mission Major Risner is to establish a network of reliable contacts and intelligence sources to give us the heads-up that we need to counter the North Vietnamese Army's next move. I don't want to lose any of those aircraft in Chu Lai, but particularly the A-6s and F-4s. Those A-6s from Da Nang and Chu Lai are doing a great job of bombing up north. I read those Bomb Damage Assessment reports every day and they are impressive. "

Standing up, Major General Walt extended his hand to Major Risner, "Good luck Rich, I know you're the man that I need."

"Thank you Sir, you can count on me."

Taking that as his cue that the meeting was over, Major Risner braced himself at attention and was preparing to execute the proper dismissing form of taking three paces backwards then executing an about face when the General interrupted, "By the way Major Risner, you performed a valuable service in Korea. Your country owes you a debt of gratitude."

"Thank you, Sir" and with that he took three steps backwards, did an about face and left.

Lieutenant Colonel Corson

Lieutenant Colonel William R. Corson greeted Major Risner like he was meeting an old friend. Corson was serving on back-to-back tours of duty of 13 months each but had the enthusiasm and eagerness of a newly graduated Marine from Boot Camp. Extending his hand he pumped Risner's like trying to prime an old water pump.

"Glad as hell you are here, Major. Welcome aboard."

"Thank you, Sir it's good to be here."

"I know you have been briefed by General Walt. What do you think of him?"

"I am very impressed by his knowledge of what is going on and what he is trying to accomplish."

"Yes I agree. Did he say anything to you about the scholarship program?"

"No, he did not. What scholarship program?"

"I'm not surprised. He is not the type to brag. We found soon after our arrival in country that the overwhelming majority of families are in extreme poverty conditions. Average income in the Chu Lai area is around $5.00 per month. To put that into the proper perspective, a live chicken sold for food at an open market costs $5.00. That means that fresh meat is a luxury and the main staple is fish and rice. A family can plant their own rice and catch their own fish without charge if they have the means. The unintended consequence of this is that the average family needs the children to help with the farming and work where possible, just to put food on the table. The villagers who lived in the area where Chu Lai Combat Base is now located were all moved outside the perimeter of the base to what is known as the Chu Lai New Life Hamlet. Marines and Sailors helped them to make the move and built some rudimentary structures so they could have a market place and fresh water facilities. Most of their homes are held together by a combination of scrap metal, fabric and lean-to type tents. Those that can afford it have brick type structures made the old fashioned way of hand making bricks. The bricks are more sand than gravel and will only last a few months or years as the Monsoon seasons erode them away. They have to replant and establish new crops in this sandy crap we call dirt."

"Sounds pretty grim."

"It is. If that cycle is not rectified there will soon be a generation of Vietnamese that are no better off than their ancestors by not being able to read or write. So General Walt began a scholarship program that we have named after him where a Marine will sponsor a Vietnamese child for $5.00 a month. These children are nominated by the Village Elders, Chiefs and religious leaders. The child's picture is taken with a short biographical description of the child and is made into a scholarship application. The Village Chief or Elder signs the document attesting to family's poverty situation and the CAP units seek out Marine volunteers to sponsor a child. The sponsor receives a copy of the picture and the scholarship form. They in turn are sending some of these applications to the States where local communities are adopting children or in some cases a school to sponsor. The money is paid directly each month to the families of sponsored children to make sure that no one gets in the middle to try and siphon it off. To get the program going General Walt personally sponsored a large number of children to begin with and now he has sponsored over 15 children himself. I am proud to say that every CAP unit in I Corps has 100 percent participation amongst the CAP members. That means a typical Private with a base pay of $87.50 plus hostile fire pay and overseas allowance is pulling in somewhere around $150.00 or less per month and yet he is sponsoring at least one child and many are sponsoring two or more. It's unbelievable what the response has been. We're hoping you can achieve similar results with all of the Marines we have in Chu Lai. No child should be denied school because their family needs them for work."

"I agree" replied Risner. "This sounds like something that we can really use to bolster our support with the locals as well as our military. I'm behind it 100 percent."

"Thanks, that what I want to hear. Let me fill you in on some of the details of what we are doing and what our successes and failures have been to date. How about a cup of coffee?" he asked.

"Thought you would never ask," Risner said smiling.

For the next two hours Corson and Risner went over the standard operating procedures Corson had put together for the CAP units. Corson explained the reporting requirements as well as goals set for each of the units. Risner commented that he recognized a lot of what was being done from what he had read and studied from the Marine Corps Small Wars Manual of 1940. This was adopted from the Marine Corps experience in the "Banana Wars" fought in the Caribbean.

"Did you know that General Walt was trained by some of these Marine veterans of deployments to Nicaragua, Haiti and the Dominican Republic?" Risner shook his head no but knew about the methods used for civil development and training of militia from the manual. The manual stated in part: "In regular warfare, the responsible officers simply strive to attain a method of producing the maximum physical effect with the force at their disposal. In small wars, the goal is to gain decisive results with the least application of force and the consequent minimum loss of life. The end aim is the social, economic, and political development of the people subsequent to the military defeat of the enemy insurgent forces. In small wars, tolerance, sympathy, and kindness should be the keynote of our relationship with the mass of the population."

"This is definitely counter to what current Military Assistance Command Vietnam policy is, am I correct?" Risner asked.

Corson smiled, "If by MACV you mean General Westmoreland you are exactly right."

He continued, "Our Marines are largely dependent upon themselves and their PF trainees for their very lives. They are all volunteers and each one faces extreme danger every day they are in the field. They know that by the time they need the Cavalry to appear it may be too late. We have suffered many casualties but our percentage numbers are still less than the conventional forces. So we operate on the 'lean' both in the CAP units as well as our larger forces. Westmoreland will not staff the CAP units independently from our Division elements. To be fair I know he understands the importance of what we do but he thinks it takes too long to accomplish. He refuses to acknowledge what we have already learned from captured intelligence: that Hanoi is willing to send two new men from North Vietnam for every man lost in the South. Hell, we've found, captured or killed hundreds if not thousands of North Vietnamese Army soldiers as young as 13 or 14 and they have used kids as young as 5 or 6 as sappers (suicide bombers) both boys and girls. They just keep replacing them. We're finding that many are hopped up on marijuana or heroin before they begin their assaults. How do you defend against that other than to wipe them out?" Corson grimaced. "How do we tell our friends and families that we have to kill pregnant women and young boys or girls being used as pawns in this war? The answer is we can't. Some day everyone must know but in the interim we have to fight the only way we know how and the Army has decided that way to be massive armed force engagements that don't discriminate between young and old, male or female, friend or foe. If they are in the way they will be decimated."

Corson shrugged his shoulders as if to say there

was no answer, then said, "For every 10 good deeds we do, it can be undone by one reckless act. Whether it's an aircraft dropping napalm on the wrong village or a soldier shooting innocent civilians thinking them to be Viet Cong, it makes no difference. After a while the locals don't care who the good guys are supposed to be they just want the damn thing to be over. That's why we can't give up. Once we embed our Marines in the villages they are there to provide the security, training and necessary civic action projects to bring the people to our side and that of their own government. Do you know that before we came in country, there was no television or radio or newspapers throughout the entire country? We now have Armed Forces Vietnam Network radio and TV emanating from both DaNang and Saigon. Every day we are getting TVs and radios supplied to local villages and hamlets so they can see and hear programming for both Vietnamese and English audiences. They get the news from Saigon and special programs and soap operas in their own language and then we have programming for the troops that can receive it. It starts around 1600 and continues until 2000. We also have the PSYOPS (Psychological Operations) guys come into the bigger villages and set-up 16mm movies for everyone. For most it is the first time they have ever seen a motion picture. The kids love it when they show the short cartoons. All of this is being done to try and unify these people with their government." Corson paused for a moment. "Need a refill on that coffee? I do." Risner nodded his head yes. After refilling both their cups from a small percolating pot, Corson continued.

"We have at least one Corpsman attached to each CAP unit. When we are able we try to get regular doctors and dentists to go with us under the protection of our CAP units. God bless the Navy for their brave young men who serve alongside us. They wear the same uniform except for their rating designation and that caduceus. They are considered as Marines by all of us as they put their lives on the line along with us. The doctors and dentists do what the Corpsmen can't so that's usually the more serious problems. They teach all of the villagers good hygiene practices. We teach them water purification and sanitation. We show them how to pour concrete bases around their wells to prevent dirty and soapy water from re-entering the wells. We try to provide materials for new school additions through CARE (Cooperative for Assistance and Relief Everywhere) and USAID (United States Agency for International Development) but unfortunately a lot of that material gets siphoned off before we ever get a chance to use it." At this Corson paused for a moment giving Risner a chance to say something.

"Why isn't all this being reported stateside Colonel?" Risner asked.

"Because it is not as important as the daily body count of our young men and the number of enemy killed in action. Most of the reporters at this point in the War are looking for reasons to get us out of here. They search for the dissenters, the complainers, the ones doing drugs, using the War as an excuse for their pitiful lack of conscience and duty. They (reporters) know as you and I and Generals Krulak and Walt know that sooner or later the American people are going to tire of this War and demand we get out. I can assure you that General Giap, the NVA Commander is taking note of all this negative coverage and he takes great delight in showing Jane Fonda and all the other flower children how much this War is costing the United States in money, materials and bodies. He is just waiting us out. The good that we are doing here is widely unreported as it does not fit into the plans set forth by the Army in its search and destroy philosophy nor does it help the agenda of our left-wing critics like Senator Proxmire of Wisconsin."

Corson rose and beckoned Risner to join him as they went outside Corson's office. Directly in front of them was a platoon of Popular Forces, about 30 men marching in formation. Leading them was a Marine Sergeant who was barking out the orders as they marched.

"Left, left, left adel-left, left, left adel-left" the sounds of which sounded almost like a song; a song known well to all Marines who have been through boot camp.

"Column right, march! Column left, march! To the rear, March! Platoon, halt! Right face!" They were now facing the Sergeant in front of them who had his back to Colonel Corson and Major Risner.

"Present........arms!" At this command each one of the soldiers raised their right hands to their black berets in a hand salute. The Marine Sergeant executed a smart about face and rendered his own hand salute.

To Colonel Corson he barked out "Platoon is ready for inspection, Sir!" Both Corson and Risner snapped to attention. As Corson was the senior officer it was his duty to return the salute not Risner. Corson returned the salute and said "Thank you Sergeant Dominic. As you were."

The Sergeant lowered his hand to his side but not before saying "Aye, Aye Sir!"

Executing another smart about face the Sergeant said to the platoon: "Order........arms!" and each one of the soldiers brought their hands back to their sides.

"At ease!" the Sergeant barked. "Smoking lamp is lit."

The Sergeant marched up to the two Marine Officers snapped to attention and rendered the proper salute. This time it was returned by both officers as is the military custom.

"Sergeant Dominic, I want you to meet Major Risner." He said. Risner extended his hand to the Sergeant. "Excellent work, Sergeant" Risner offered.

"Thank you Sir" was the response. "It has taken 2 weeks just to get this far but now that we have molded them as a unit, my fellow CAP member Sergeant Ortiz and I will teach them basic weapons use and tactics. We are trying to get them ready to deploy with only 4 weeks of training so we have a lot remaining." Looking at Risner, the Sergeant said "It's an honor to meet you sir."

"Likewise" Risner replied.

Rendering a hand salute to both officers, Dominic said "By your leave, Sir."

Corson replied "Carry on Sergeant Dominic. Outstanding job as usual." And he returned the salute.

"Thank you, Sir" was the reply. The Sergeant executed an about face and marched back to the PFs.

"I wanted you to see this Rich along with some of the other training performed here. The difference between here and the CAP units is that we are attached to the base at Da Nang so we can train local Popular Forces here until we're ready to put them out on the perimeters of their villages. Our remote CAP units have to do it all while protecting them without any other type of support. So we teach them everything we can concerning small arms tactics and defense. In turn they teach us their language and customs and help us root out the good guys from the bad guys inside the villages. We rely on them heavily because it is the Village elders or chiefs who tell us who we can trust. We must gain their confidence and bring them together as a people trained to defend themselves and to keep the enemy out thus denying him sanctuary. There-in lays the root of the problem."

"What do you mean, Sir?" Risner asked.

"We are so busy trying to accomplish the military objectives that we hardly have enough time to perform Civic Action projects that are needed. We've already discussed all the things we try to do for these people but the emphasis has to be on training the Popular Forces to defend the villages if we can ever hope to extract our forces. If we leave before that happens, the Viet Cong and North Vietnamese Army will come back and kill all the elders, chieftains and their families in retaliation for helping us, the Americans. Unfortunately it is happening every day even with some of the villages that have CAP units embedded. However, the numbers are decreasing as our CAP forces gain more confidence and loyalty from the Popular Forces and the villagers. To make it all work we have to do a better job of helping them with their infrastructure and personal needs and by learning their language and customs. We have tried to find as many of the Defense Language Institute grads as we can to volunteer for the CAP units. You will probably find some in Chu Lai that will help you as you set up your Civic Action Team. And that brings me full circle as to why you are here. Let's go back to my office."

As they walked into Corson's office he led Major Risner to one of his wall maps of I Corps that looked identical to General Walt's maps.

"I know that you've probably seen this in Walt's office" he said.

"Yes Sir I have."

"Good, because it is my job to keep his updated with mine."

"Where do we get the numbers from?" Risner asked.

"Good question" Corson replied. Everything that comes into my office is provided by Division Intelligence Officers, both Marine Corps and Army. For you in Chu Lai that will be Americal Division Intelligence. They provide daily and weekly intelligence reports that show me what areas are considered hostile by day or night or, both."

"Where do they get their numbers from?" Risner countered.

"Another good question. Our Marine numbers come from RECON units' (Reconnaissance) reports and the Army numbers come from LRRP (Long Range Reconnaissance Patrols) reports. It is my job to take those reports and marry them with input I get from each of my CAP Officers in Charge or Army Civil Affairs Officers in Charge. As you can see from the Chu Lai area of our map we have a lot to do. Work closely with Americal Division and the local CAP units. We need to get better intelligence on what Charley is up to, especially for TET. You can accomplish what we cannot in your area: perform Civic Action projects that will bring the people over to our side, thus providing more and better informants. You will have some funds at your disposal to accomplish that mission. Just be careful because, as you probably know, money can often buy bad intelligence rather than good. Be prepared to be dealing with both friendly and enemy contacts. You can never be entirely sure who you are dealing with until you can get to know them. You have to be the judge. I would suggest meeting with as many local officials and CAP units as you can and get the program rolling. The CAP units will appreciate your assistance as they are tied up full time trying to train the Popular Forces to defend themselves. As General Walt probably told you, you are writing the book on this effort. You have to exercise your gut feelings a lot and remember our end goal. General Walt has placed special confidence in you and so have I. I'll get down there to visit with you when I can. Semper Fi and good luck, Rich."

"Thank you, Sir," Risner replied as he left Corson's office.

ASSIGNMENT CHU LAI

"Major Risner, welcome aboard!" Lieutenant Colonel Bob Barton said as he came from behind his desk to greet the newly assigned officer and shook Rich's hand. "Call me Bob, please. I understand you go by Rich."

"Yes sir, I do. Thank you."

"I know you flew in from DaNang last night and you got checked into the temporary Officer's Quarters. Have you been assigned a permanent hooch?"

"Yes sir, thank you, I'm sharing one with Major Durham."

"Major Durham? Hope you like scotch! That's his favorite. He's a damn fine A-4 pilot as well as our Group Operations Officer. Please, have a chair." Barton pulled his chair off to the side so that he was sitting next to Risner.

"Sorry I can't introduce you to the Group Skipper but he's out on a strike sortie right now. Between flying one of the A-4s and the Hummer he's not around very much so I end up covering the Group for him. The Hummer is the aircraft you flew in on last night piloted by Captain R.C. Moore, the Operations Officer for Headquarters and Maintenance Squadron. I know you are an infantry officer so you are probably not that familiar with our designations but you'll catch on fast, I know." Barton went on to explain the mission of the Group and individual squadrons.

"There are two aircraft groups based at Chu Lai.

Marine Aircraft Group 13 has all the F-4 Phantom aircraft including the RF-4B a recon/photo bird and some old TF-9Js left over from the Korean War as training aircraft. Marine Aircraft Group 12 has all the A-4 Skyhawks as well as the A-6A Intruder and EA-6B Electronic Countermeasures (ECM) Prowlers. The Intruders are used to bomb targets in the DMZ as well as limited targets in Haiphong Harbor and North Vietnam. The ECM aircraft are there to jam enemy radar signals used by surface to air missiles for guidance as well as jam any other communications used by the enemy. The A-6A's carry up to 36 of the 500 pound bombs. The North Vietnamese Army and the Viet Cong are always trying to target the A-6s in Da Nang and Chu Lai using B40 and 122mm rockets."

Barton went explained the layout of the base using a detailed map labeled Chu Lai Combat Base behind his desk. The map showed that the far North end of the base jutted out like a small peninsula. Directly across by less than a kilometer was Ky Xuan Island. On the peninsula was an Army surgical hospital with a large helicopter landing pad used by Medical Evacuation or more commonly known as the MEDEVAC helicopters. The inland port of Chu Lai located adjacent to the hospital was run by the U.S. Navy and was known as the Sand Ramp or Naval Supply Activity Depot. This was also where the Seabees Construction Battalion was located. Due west of the peninsula across from the Sand Ramp was the base perimeter where the village of Sam Hai was located.

"Most of the Vietnamese club and mess hall workers come and go every day through this gate manned by Americal Division Military Police with a few sailors and Marines assigned as an augmented force," Barton explained.

He went on to say that due south from the peninsula comprising the larger portion of the base was Americal Division Headquarters and the Army billeting area. Here the main Post Exchange was located as well as an amphitheater where Bob Hope brought his Christmas Show to perform every year. The past Christmas of 1966, Bob had brought Ann Margret much to the delight of all.

The Americal Division was bordered on the east by the South China Sea. To the west was the perimeter about 5 kilometers away. Following along the coast further south of Americal Division was a small USO facility as well as billeting areas for the Air Force 20th Tactical Air Support Squadron and the Army 21st Reconnaissance Aircraft Company. Immediately south of these units was the Marine Aircraft Group 12 billeting area. The further most northern area was Officers' Country occupied by the Officers' Mess, the Officers' Club and several tent hooches. A road ran parallel with the ocean beach a couple of hundred yards to the west separating the club and mess from the living quarters. Going further west was the Group and Headquarters and Maintenance Squadron headquarters. Further down the beach about one kilometer was the enlisted billeting area. Here was located the Staff Non-Commissioned Officer's Club, the Sergeant's Club and the Enlisted Club as well as the Enlisted Mess Hall. The Staff Non-Commissioned Officers had their own billeting area closest to the beach. Across the road further west were the Post Exchange and Concession buildings. The rest of the enlisted were billeted south and across the road to the west. Going further west was the Supply buildings. Following the road to the southernmost area of Marine Aircraft Group 12 was the Motor transport section and maintenance buildings; continuing south were the Mobile Construction Battalion 40 (Seabees) and the Fuel Tank Farm. On the furthest south of the base were Americal Military Intelligence Division and the Long Range Reconnaissance Patrol headquarters.

Directly across from the Group Headquarters was a SATS Field (Short Aircraft Tactical Strip) made of metal interlocking planks or matting. This strip was approximately 2 kilometers long and was marked with revetments used to house and protect a Marine A-4 squadron as well as the Army and Air Force spotter Aircraft and the Ch-47 Chinook helicopters belonging to the 1st Air Cav and elements of the 101st Airborne Division. This was a secondary airfield to the main airfield. About 5-10 kilometers to the west from the enlisted living area were the main runways that ran North to South and one Northeast to Southwest. To the south of the main runway were the Bomb Dump and Explosive Ordnance Disposal and the southern perimeter of the base. Barton went on to explain the interaction or lack thereof between the Army and the Marine Corps concerning base defenses.

"Since our Marine Infantry units left followed by Marine Aircraft Group 36 and all of their helicopters, the Army has taken over the base EXCEPT the Air Base. Chu Lai Air Base is part of the overall Chu Lai Combat Base. So we requested an on-site Marine Infantry officer who could keep our asses safe. We have to provide our own security so we have a Group Guard of which you are the new Commanding Officer. These men will be assigned in a random manner for a 30 day period of duty. Every enlisted man here is required to perform at least one support duty function during a 13 month tour of duty. There are three of these: mess duty, guard duty and police duty. Mess and guard are self-explanatory. Police duty is carried out by the Police Sergeant who takes care of the daily ritual of burning off the shitters and making sure the living areas are kept clean and safe. Now I think you can figure out who gets assigned to these details when the Officers In Charge are given quotas. You can bet that the best technicians and mechanics remain on the flight line and are not assigned to these details."

Risner chuckled. "So I'll getting the cream of the crap, I mean crop."

Barton laughed also. "You got it right the first time. Seriously though, you will get to pick your team as long as I don't have to compromise aircraft readiness. Just as you have to account on a daily basis what your operational readiness is with your infantry unit so do I with aircraft readiness."

Barton continued, "If you look at the strategic layout of this base as I am sure you already have

(Risner was nodding assent), it is very difficult for Charley to mass any kind of ground force without it being detected far in advance. The terrain between us and Da Nang to the north is flat and devoid of jungle growth along Route 1, the main service road. Chu Lai is set in the middle of a sand bowl that extends at least a couple of kilometers around the entire base. Most of the damage that we receive is from intermittent mortar attacks that really aren't practical or effective because of the close-in range or B40 and 122mm rockets fired from a maximum range of 5-7 kilometers. It's pretty much a hit and miss calculation. They hope they get lucky and hit one of our aircraft. Small numbers of well trained sappers are a different story and that is why we need an effective Group Guard, mainly during the night hours. In any event how and when they are deployed is now up to you."

"I'm looking forward to it" Risner replied.

"I know you met with Corson. Did you get any ideas from him? General Walt speaks highly of him."

"And rightly so. I think if the Army was trying to pursue the same strategy that we (the Marines) are we might have a chance of winning this War."

"Haven't you read the Stars and Stripes? (An in-country newspaper edited by the military) Westmoreland says we are winning," Barton said smiling.

"I must have missed that edition." Replied Risner.

"Well according to General Walt, I am to give you or get you whatever you need to accomplish your objectives. You will probably have to use your own wit and charm to get what you need from the Navy and Army but I'll help where I can. My sense of all this tells me your primary duty as Ground Defense Officer will really be your collateral duty and the CAP function will be your primary. Speaking of which what are we going to call your unit? Another CAP?"

"No, Sir. I want to call it the Marine Aircraft Group 12 Civic Action Team. It's appropriate because we will not be an embedded unit in the villages and hamlets and our primary focus will be on performing civic actions. If we can win the hearts and minds, as the saying goes, the rest will follow."

Smiling, Barton said "I thought it was Chesty Puller who said if you grab them by the balls, the hearts and minds will follow."

Risner laughed. "I know. I had the honor and privilege of meeting him once at Camp Pendleton at the Officer's Club. He is bigger than life and the epitome of what being a Marine Officer is about."

Every Marine who goes through Boot Camp learns Marine Corps history from 1775 to present. Chesty Puller, actually named Lewis B. Puller, was the most decorated Marine in Marine Corps History and the only Marine to earn 5 Navy Crosses, the Nation's second highest award to the Medal of Honor.

"I think we all agree on that. By the way, don't be surprised if right after TAPS is played around 2200, you hear someone yelling into the night 'Goodnight Chesty, wherever you are!'" Risner laughed with him.

Turning serious, Risner continued "I have been

working a plan in my head and I will put pen to paper beginning tomorrow to give you an idea of where I want to start and what I'll need."

Barton: "Just let me know. By the way one of the men you requested is on the way here from Okinawa according to a Naval Message I got today, Staff Sergeant Petterson."

Risner smiled "We go back together to Korea."

Barton: "Good, just let me know how many others you need."

"Thank you, Sir."

STAFF SERGEANT PETTERSON

"Staff Sergeant Richard M. Petterson, that's with 2 T's, reporting as ordered, Sir!" He barked out.

"Dick, what took you so long?" Risner asked smiling. Rising from behind his desk he went around to Petterson to shake his hand. Staff Sergeant Petterson hailed from Washington, D.C. and was around 5'10" tall with a lean physique. When he spoke he had an eastern accent with a rich baritone voice that reminded Risner of Humphrey Bogart. Friendly by nature but guarded about his personal life he embodied the picture of the ideal Marine Staff NCO. He could be your best friend or your worst enemy.

"Punched anyone out today, Sir?" Petterson asked smiling.

Risner smiling back said, "No, but the day's not over. Tell me what you have been doing."

Petterson explained how he had received word that Risner was looking for him. "The damn CG at El Toro called me into his office and wanted to know how I was connected to the Commandant to receive special orders without him knowing about it!"
Petterson smiled, "Of course I played dumb and that just made him madder. After he figured out that I wasn't going to educate him he sent me on my way. So what's going on here and why are you not assigned to an infantry unit?"

Risner explained his meeting with Walt and the charge he was given. "I want you to be my NCOIC and get this unit operational as soon as possible."

"Sounds interesting, I'm ready to go."

For the next few days both combed through the lists provided by Walt for those Marines in country who had been through the Defense Language Institute Vietnamese Language Training. They found 6 enlisted Marines between the 2 air groups that had completed the training. Of those they interviewed four who had at least 10 months or more remaining on their 13 month tours of duty. Of those they selected one: Corporal Gene Hays.

Sergeant Randy Coleman who was a DLI graduate was chosen even though he only had 3 months left on his tour because he possessed the language skills and had a good working relationship with most of the Vietnamese workers on base. Corporal Doug McKillips and Private First Class Garry Williams had not been through language training but were selected because of their availability and good recommendations from their superiors.

The Third Marine Division in Da Nang assigned Sgt Dan Bowman who was not trained in the language but was a Nuclear, Biological, and Chemical Warfare specialist. General Walt thought that such a Marine would be useful to the Marines in Chu Lai in the event of a ground attack. In the meanwhile the Army of the Republic of Vietnam Headquarters in Saigon assigned a Vietnamese Marine Staff Sergeant named Phan Thanh Cong as an interpreter. Staff Sergeant Cong was 30 years old, married and had 5 children. Prior to his induction into the Vietnamese Marine Corps he had been an architect and building contractor in Saigon. His family lived in modest accommodations in the Cholon sector of Saigon that was the Chinese district. During the years that Vietnam was under French dominance, the French language was a second language for Cong and most of the other residents. Cong's wife was a cousin of the royal family that once ruled his country from Hue City and was also fluent in French. Risner knew that Cong's engineering expertise would help with the civic action projects he had planned.

Sergeant Randy Coleman was just a good old boy raised on a farm in Pennsylvania. His good looks and charms made him popular with the ladies and he had a natural affinity for children.

Sergeant Dan Bowman of Rochester New York was constantly complaining about being assigned to the Air Wing but was not so vocal about it when out in the 'Ville trying to score. His primary offering to the team was the support of his Catholic Church and parish back home for the Dong Ha Orphanage as well as support from the local school systems with school supplies for the Vietnamese schools.

Corporal Gene Hays hailed from Odessa Texas and he proved to be a natural for typing reports, keeping files organized and running the daily administration duty required. His Vietnamese language skills helped when Cong was not with the unit or was assigned elsewhere.

Corporal Doug McKillips was from Portland Oregon and his main asset was his size and ability to defend himself and his other Marine brothers in a fight.

He was a natural arbiter knowing what to say and when to say it most effectually.

Private First Class Garry Williams was an Irish boy from Jersey City New Jersey. His main priorities in life were drinking, scoring with the ladies and drinking? All together Risner felt that he had the workings of a first class team. Petterson thought he would have his hands full just keeping them from killing each other or him by accident.

"Alright, listen up!" Staff Sergeant Petterson hollered above the dull roar. "Major Risner will be here in about 5 minutes to give you a briefing. I've asked that we have a Corpsman present in case I have to hurt one of you for interrupting the Major."

Everyone laughed and Petterson smiled. Turning to the Corpsman, Petterson said: "Doc Johnson here just came back from a six month tour with 3/3 up north. He's still recovering from some shrapnel wounds but has volunteered his time while he is in a recuperating status. Semper Fi Doc." That prompted an ooooooooooooohrahhhhhh!! from the other Marines.

"The Major is going to outline what we are going to be doing over the next few months. I'll be deciding who does what, along with the Major, as well as the how and when. We have a chance here to do some really meaningful work as opposed to burning off shitters, filling sandbags or washing dishes which I will gladly assign you to do if you get lazy."

About that time a jeep pulled up alongside the Office hut. "Stand by, Marines" Petterson said. All of the Marines leaned forward on their chairs anticipating the next command. Staff Sergeant Petterson stood alongside Major Risner's desk waiting for the Major to make his appearance. As the screen door was pulled open Petterson barked out, "Marines, atent......hut!!"

The massive body of Major Risner stooped a little to keep from hitting his head on the door jamb and as he entered the office he said, "At ease, Gentlemen, as you were." Striding towards his desk he nodded at Staff Sergeant Petterson "Thank you, Staff Sergeant Petterson, please continue." And he sat down behind his desk. Only after he sat did the other enlisted Marines take their seats.

"As I was saying gentlemen you have a chance to be part of an elite unit. Make sure you don't do or say anything to screw that up. I'm now going to turn this meeting over to Major Risner." Waiting for the Major to rise, Staff Sergeant Petterson stood beside his chair. When Risner stood up he walked to the side of his desk opposite from Petterson and half-sat on the corner of his desk. Petterson then sat in his chair.

"The Staff Sergeant is absolutely correct Gentlemen. I expect each and every one of you to look your best at all times and to avoid doing anything that could bring disgrace or dishonor to this unit. That means if you want to have a Vietnamese girlfriend wait until you go on R&R (Rest and Relaxation Leave) to China Beach in Da Nang or better yet don't get hooked up with some one that you will give you a gift that you won't want to return home with." Risner smiled as the men laughed. "Most importantly remember to look out for one another and do not put yourself in unnecessary dangerous situations. We will be spending most of our day light hours working with the Vietnamese people. You will have to set the example by your appearance and actions. Staff Sergeant Petterson and I have spent a lot of time with Americal Division G2. That is their Division Intelligence unit for those of you who are wondering. Based on after-action reports, first hand intelligence from the LRRPs and paid informants, we have a good idea of the areas that are pacified or not. Staff Sergeant Petterson, if you will?"

Risner motioned to an easel beside Petterson that was turned backwards. Petterson brought the easel to the front and turned it around making the front sheet of light brown paper visible to all. The cover sheet read in bold letters: "MAG-12 CIVIC ACTION TEAM."

"That is the name of our unit," Risner said pointing to the easel.

"That name is already painted on the sides of the two vehicles that we now own: a Jeep and a Cerlist (3/4 Ton Pickup with engine mounted in the middle). That identifies who we are while we are out in the 'Ville and that makes us a target for our enemies. Now you might be wondering why we would want to advertise our presence. First, it shows that we are not afraid to be out there. Second, if we do our job well the locals will probably protect us if they believe we are there to help them. Third, it identifies you from all of the rest of the uniforms out there as belonging to an elite and trusted unit. When we go out in the 'Ville we will be wearing our soft covers and basic Table of Organization weapon. If we travel by military convoy or if we are travelling though unknown territory we will wear flak jackets and helmets. Bottom line is we want to keep a low profile while we quietly go about our business. And this point is absolutely paramount to us doing our duty: we provide the materials and know how but the Vietnamese people do the work and receive the credit for it. We will monitor and supervise and dole out materials as needed, ensuring that all materials are being used for their intended purpose but we will not do the work. This is a Self-Help Program that I want to implement from the start."

Heads nodded in understanding as the Major paused and went over to the water cooler to get a cup of water. Staff Sergeant Petterson picked up as if on cue flipping the sheet over on the easel. It was labeled "CIVIC ACTION PROJECTS."

"We will get our materials from any source we can. That means the Seabees, the Army, the Vietnamese government as well as CARE and USAID from the States." Flipping over the next sheet, it was labeled "SCHOOL SUPPLIES."

"Sergeant Bowman has agreed to write to a lot of people in his home town of Rochester New York. We are asking them to send us pencils, pens, notebook paper and any other school supplies that may be needed."

Flipping over the next chart, it was labeled "ORPHANAGES."

"Dan also has his local Catholic parish contributing clothing and other donations to the Dong Ha Catholic Orphanage and the Dickie Chapelle

Memorial Hospital. For those of you who don't know who Chapelle is, she was the first female war correspondent killed in Vietnam almost a year ago. The rest of you need to write your relatives and friends and get them to organize donations for school supplies and clothing. I have some sheets typed out with suggested items for donation that I will pass out at the end of this briefing. For everything we receive we will send back a Certificate of Appreciation thanking them for helping the MAG-12 Civic Action Team and the Vietnamese people." Again as if on cue, Petterson sat down and Risner continued.

"Next," Risner said, which was the cue for Petterson to flip the next chart labeled "GENERAL WALT SCHOLARSHIP PROGRAM." He went on to explain the program as Lieutenant Colonel Corson had explained to him.

"I want you to get sponsors from back home any way that you can. We have 500 scholarship papers ready for sponsors. Staff Sergeant Petterson will be in charge of the scholarship funds and Corporal Hays will provide a dual accountability function. I will conduct monthly audits myself. I have initiated an order from the Group Executive Officer, Lieutenant Colonel Barton to all of the Squadron Commanders directing them to form 5 man Civic Action Teams for each squadron in MAG-12. These men will all be volunteers and will be performing these functions as collateral duties. The Squadrons include VMA(AW)-533, VMA-121, VMA-211, VMA-311 and VMA-223. That's an additional 25 men who will be scrounging materials for us and trying to find sponsors for our school kids. Next."

Petterson flipped the chart again. The new chart read: "SELF-HELP PROGRAM."

"Using the Village Chiefs, Elders and religious leaders, we will identify needs within the villages for new schools, school additions, market facilities, temples, churches, medical clinics and any other infrastructure needed. Staff Sergeant Cong will be in charge of this program and he will verify all of the building needs as far as men and material. He will help supervise but the local villagers will perform the labor and will take ownership of the project as it is being built through completion and final occupation.

"Next," Risner said.

Petterson flipped the chart again. The new chart read: "MEDICAL, DENTAL AND SANITATION PROJECTS."

"This is self-explanatory as far as the medical and dental. Doc Johnson is going to accompany us to every new village and hamlet we go. He'll be carrying the normal first-aid supplies but he'll also have bar soap, toothbrushes and toothpaste, water purification tablets and a host of other basic medicines used to treat everything from head lice to toe fungus. He will help us explain the need for cement bases around the wells to keep dirty/soapy water from re-entering the well water. He will teach them basic sanitation procedures. We will get volunteer Doctors and Dentists from time to time to help us as needed."

Risner returned to his chair and Petterson took

the lead.

"Part of the medical assistance we will provide will be to help amputees. We found out from one of the local nurses at the Chapelle Clinic that the Quakers operate a medical facility in Quang Ngai about 35 clicks (kilometers) to the south. In case you are not aware the Quakers oppose all wars and will not fight. I'm told that it is an amazing place because the nationality or uniform worn by the patients make no difference to the Quakers. All sides are bound by this neutrality and the amazing thing is that everyone honors it. We will identify children first as a priority for needing artificial limbs. After them come adults of any age needing prosthetics. We will provide the transportation to and from the clinic." Flipping the next chart Petterson pointed to it and read: "PEOPLE TO PEOPLE PROGRAM."

"This is what we are about as Marines and Civic Action Team members. We are waging a new and different kind of war: that of winning the hearts and minds of the people. It is a noble effort that is sometimes criticized by our own brothers in arms as well as those from the other branches of service. Be aware of it, be sensitive to it but do not allow yourself to get drawn in to a 'kill them all' mentality. We strive to identify the good from the bad but sometimes we will not know who we are dealing with. Learn the language, observe their customs and treat them with the respect our own culture and morals dictate. You should also realize that many of them have been or will be victimized by the NVA and VC if they help us. That is why we will follow up with the local CAP units and other ground forces to provide them with defensive training and protection where we are able to do so. By befriending them we can gain valuable intelligence needed for our own defenses as well as theirs. So be vigilant, observant, polite and ask questions when you don't understand. Hopefully they will respond in kind by giving us intelligence and protection." Petterson sat down.

"Well said, Staff Sergeant Petterson. I think we're done for now. I look forward to working with all of you. I leave you now in the very capable hands of Staff Sergeant Petterson."

"Atten....hut!" Petterson barked. Everyone stood at attention as Major Risner headed towards the door.

"As you were Gentlemen." Risner said on the way out.

MEETING WITH PHAM AND WITH KHOI

Mr. Pham was the Village Chief for An Tan, the village just outside the main gate from Chu Lai. Highway 1 split the village in two going north to Da Nang and South to Quang Ngai. Nguyen Van Pham was a former Viet Minh soldier in the fight against French Occupation for ten years. The Viet Minh were supported by the new Chinese Communist government who also supported Ho Chi Minh as the newly appointed Prime Minister of North Vietnam after the French agreed to leave Vietnam in 1954. Many of the former Viet Minh did not want to live under the Communist rule and therefore left North Vietnam to live in South Vietnam. The intent of the Chinese was that Ho Chi Minh would take over the entire country but the nation ended up being split in two at the 17th parallel with unifying elections to be held in 1956. But Pham and other Viet Minh who fled North Vietnam for a democratic state in South Vietnam never agreed to the partition or the proposed elections knowing that Ho Chi Minh, with the backing of the Chinese would assume Communist control of all of Vietnam.

The Viet Minh became the NLF or National Liberation Front. Allied while fighting the French, the splintered Viet Minh became bitter enemies over the split between a socialist state and a democratic state. Pham kept in touch with some of his former friends in the North and from time to time would learn what they were doing and more importantly what they were

65

planning. It seems both sides were playing a cat and mouse game, neither willing to place all of their bets on one outcome. The truth was that no matter how optimistic the leaders of both sides were as to who would prevail in the long run, the minions were not so sure and they wanted to be on the winning side regardless of the consequences. Pham played the game with finesse, trading information that was already known to the other side but still good enough to keep his contacts open in the North. What set Pham apart from the others was that he would never bow to the Communist North. Known only to his closest family members, two of whom remained in North Vietnam was his vitriolic hatred of the NLF for the senseless murder of his wife and three children in Hanoi in retaliation for his defection to the South. He would regret not taking them with him at the time for the rest of his life even though he knew it would have been impossible to get them through the lines to the South. He never spoke of it to anyone until he met the "Nguoi My Thieu-ta;" the American Major named Risner. They had only met twice before but Pham sensed a kinship between the two military men from the beginning. Risner's warmth, charm and respect for Pham had Pham talking about things he had never shared with anyone: graphic details of what had happened at the Battle of Điện Biên Phủ. Risner listened and showed appreciation and understanding and shared some of his own personal life with Pham. Talking about Risner's family is what got Pham to talk about his own. Thus began a fruitful friendship for both. It soon became known throughout the area that any trouble given to one would bring down the wrath of the other. Neither knew just how far that knowledge stretched.

Mr. Khoi was the Headmaster at Ly Tin High School. Ly Tin was the District Headquarters for An Tan, Sam Hai and the Chu Lai New Life Hamlet; something comparable to a county seat in America. Khội was an intellectual who was also quite adept at getting along with everyone. He knew he was in a precarious situation as most of the other males with his education were officers in the Army of the Republic of Vietnam. Drafted soldiers were required to serve a minimum of 7 to 11 years. Khoi presented himself as apolitical but inwardly he detested socialism and correctly saw it as a threat to free thinking and therefore a threat to academia in general. Khoi had been too young to fight the French and had never lived in the North. He was married to a beautiful woman of his same age of 26 named Phương Minh. She was a direct descendant of the Nguyễn Dynasty, the last ruling family of Vietnam whose capital was Huễ City. When her father the Emperor Bảo Đại abdicated in 1945 the Communist capital was moved to Hanoi and her family fled to Saigon. During that trip, her parents who were concerned for her safety left her in the care of a cousin in Ly Tin where she grew up with Khoi and they eventually married. The family made a few trips to see relatives in Saigon but by this time her father had already been living in exile in France. Her relationship to the royal family was a closely guarded secret not even revealed to Khoi until just before their marriage. Pham introduced Khoi to Major Risner. He told Risner:

"You like him very much. He is not soldier like you and me but he is very smart." Pham said smiling. Winking his eye he added "And he has a very beautiful wife. Beauceau, (very) pretty. You see. She will have baby soon maybe 3 or 4 months."

As was the custom, men did not socialize with women especially with other married women. When Risner was taken to Khoi's house by Pham, along with Corporal Hays, both were surprised that it was a nice home even by American standards. It was sparsely furnished but tastefully arranged all in the oriental tradition of the time. Risner and Hays greeted Khoi in the traditional Buddhist way of placing the hands together as if praying and then bowing to each other. Khoi then reached forward with his hand outstretched in the American way to shake Risner's hand and then Hays' hand.

"Pleased to meet you" he said in very passable English. Risner shook his hand firmly and smiling while bending forward replied,

"The pleasure is mine, Sir."

When Hays was offered a hand, he took it and replied in Vietnamese that he was honored to meet Khoi. A look of surprise and delight came over Khoi's face as Hays spoke the words in his own native tongue and he thanked Hays.

Risner towered over all three men but his grace and manner suggested friendship. Initially they talked about the War and its effect on the local villages. Khoi reaffirmed what Risner already knew about the poverty situation and the number of children not able to attend school. Risner explained the Scholarship Program and assured him that the Marines were dedicated to supporting as many kids as possible to attend. The look of delight on Khoi's face was obvious and he offered his thanks.

"That's only the beginning Mr. Khoi" Risner said. "We hope that this increased enrollment will enable us to add on to your school and the others in this area."

As Risner was finishing his explanation of the goals of the Civic Action Team he asked Khoi how the words "Civic Action" would translate in Vietnamese. Khoi had thought for a few moments and said,

"Dan Su Vu. It loosely means civil affairs."

"Thank you" Risner replied and committed it to memory. About that same time Khoi excused himself for a moment leaving Pham and Risner alone.

"What you think?" Pham asked.

"I think I have a new friend and ally. Thank you Pham for introducing us."

Pham nodded his appreciation.

"Thieu ta (Major) Risner and Corporal Hays, please meet my wife Mrs. Khoi," Mr. Khoi announced with his wife following dutifully behind him. Risner and Hays placed their hands together and bowed.

"It is an honor Mrs. Khoi to meet you," Risner said. "You have a lovely home and I have enjoyed talking with your husband very much."

Mrs. Khoi nodded as he spoke then he suddenly

realized she didn't understand anything he was saying. Mr. Khoi quickly translated Risner's words to her and she managed to say "Thank you" in passable English. Pham jumped in by speaking French to Mrs. Khoi and she responded in French. She was startled when Risner jumped in speaking in French,

"I also speak French," and that resulted in an hour of conversation between all of them alternating between the three languages. Mrs. Khoi served hot tea to everyone along with rice bread. Speaking in French again, Risner said,

"The day is coming to a close and we need to get back before dark if possible. If it is acceptable to you, Mr. Khoi, I would like Corporal Hays to check with you at least once a week so that we may keep better informed as to the needs of your school and other matters."

Khoi knew that other matters consisted of any intelligence information he might have on enemy and friendly activities to pass on to the Team.

"We look forward to Corporal Hays' visits," Khoi replied.

"I have thoroughly enjoyed myself, Mr. and Mrs. Khoi, and your kind hospitality and look forward to meeting with you again soon." They all said their goodbyes and Pham and Risner left.

CIVIC ACTION

Over the next three months the MAG-12 Civic Action Team spent every day possible out amongst the villages and hamlets in the Chu Lai area. Major Risner, Staff Sergeant Petterson and Corporal Hays made all of the initial contacts with help from Pham and Staff Sergeant Cong who did the interpreting. Starting out to the northern most border of the Tactical Area of Responsibility they met with leaders at the Quang Ngai Province Headquarters in Tam Ky. They met with US Army advisors to the ARVNs as well as the ARVN and PF leaders. The Governor of the province was a cousin of Nguyen Cao Ky, the Vice-President of South Vietnam and had more pressing matters at hand (actually twin girls barely 16 years old) than entertaining an unknown American Marine Major. That duty fell to his ARVN Commander Lieutenant Colonel Pham Duc Hai who was busy at the time interrogating one of the Viet Cong prisoners who had surrendered under the Chieu Hoi program. This program was explained in leaflets dropped several times a month over the entire area offering amnesty for all who forsake Communism and who came over to the side of the Republic of South Vietnam and joined the ARVN military. Literally translated Chieu Hoi meant to welcome with open arms. Unfortunately for those who did cross over to the other side, they found that amnesty did not include a reprieve from beatings and torture for those who refused to cooperate by telling all about the unit they came from including what those units had planned for the future. The methods were cruel and sometimes lethal and rarely produced the desired effect as the prisoners quickly learned to make up lies as much as possible to avoid the beatings.

The US Army Advisors proved helpful by giving a tour of the area and introducing Risner and the Team to the local village chief and elders. Risner, Petterson and Hays found themselves warmly welcomed as they observed the Vietnamese customs of greeting the important men of the village. Lunch was provided at the US Army compound complete with Chinese noodles and one liter bottles of warm Ba Muoi Ba beer served with a large glass goblet containing one large chunk of ice. The Vietnamese were used to drinking warm beer but made concessions for the Americans. Corporal Hays and the others who spoke the language knew that Ba Muoi Ba translated to the number 33 but didn't realize until later that 33 represented the alcohol content of 33 percent, compared to the 3.2 percent beer they were getting back on base. Everyone was cut-off at two bottles after Risner found out. It was definitely a fun ride back to Chu Lai that night.

The next trip was to Ly Tin District Headquarters which was located between Tam Ky and Chu Lai about 6 kilometers north of Chu Lai. A US Army Advisory Group was stationed there under the command of Major Robert Nourse and was made up of 6 enlisted soldiers. Captain (Daiuy) Duoc was an ARVN Captain who commanded about 16 ARVN soldiers and about the same number of PFs. The area between Ly Tin and Tam Ky was sparsely populated but included the principal village of Ky Khoung about two kilometers further north. Major Nourse took the team there to meet with Mr. Nguyen.

Mr. Nguyen was a former Officer in the Viet Minh like Pham. When the invasion of the North Vietnamese began soon afterward, Mr. Nguyen had quit the Viet Minh and fought against the Communists fulfilling his 11-year draft requirement. Upon his discharge from the Army he returned to Ky Khoung to raise his children and live in peace. He spoke fluent French and passable English. He also manipulated a pair of manual clippers as well as any electric shears and given the choice would not use the electric ones. Major Nourse trusted him implicitly and used him frequently as a source for intelligence. Staff Sergeant Cong talked with him for a long time and was visibly impressed by the man. Cong explained later that as a former Army Officer, Nguyen still had his contacts in the military and he kept abreast of the situation around him. Unlike Pham, Mr. Nguyen did not require bribes or incentives to help the Americans; he did so freely. Mr. Nguyen was a fascinating mixture of traditional Vietnamese values and military bearing. A humble but proud man, he cared very much for his family and country. The respect given him in the village was that of a wise elder or chieftain. Mr. Nguyen had two daughters Dieu and Lan 8 and 10 years old respectively, pretty, bright and full of life. They spoke almost fluent English, a result of their schooling, their father and the few Americans they came into contact with. After a couple of weeks Dieu and Lan asked if they could come to the base and cook for the Team. They turned out to be great cooks and everyone enjoyed their company. Corporal Hays introduced them to television and they loved it. He also took them to the Seabees camp where they actually got to talk to Corporal Hays' wife on the phone and they enjoyed every minute of the conversation.

The phone calls were placed using MARS affiliates in Vietnam and in the United States. MARS is an acronym for Military Affiliate Radio System. The radio operators are HAM operators and they volunteer their services to connect servicemen and women serving overseas with their families back in the States. Most of the HAM radio connections were between Navy and Army operators stationed overseas and MARS operators in Hawaii and California. From there, the long distance charges were discounted and billed to the receiving party in the States. All calls were limited to three minutes.

Dieu and Lan especially liked the movies shown at the Rec (Recreation) Hut. Their favorite movie was The Sound of Music. It was a long movie, made longer by the projector operator starting reel 3 before reel 2. After about five minutes, realizing his mistake, it had to be rewound and reel 2 mounted. Dieu and Lan watched with fascination and delight. Their faces beamed during the scenes involving the Von Trapp children and tapped their sandals to the music. During the part when the Nazis were trying to catch them, one could see the fear and concern in the girl's eyes and their happiness at the end as they escaped. Both girls had tears streaming down their eyes at the end of the film and Corporal Hays asked why. Dieu said they cried out of happiness as they had never seen an American movie before and had never imagined how wonderful it was. They made Corporal Hays take them to that movie for the next two days it was playing.

A U.S. Navy Commander from Encinitas, California named Hartman, who was about to retire, read about the Team's work in a local newspaper story. The genesis of the story came from a letter Risner had written to the editor requesting school supplies and clothing donations for the kids in the Chu Lai area. Commander Hartman wrote Major Risner and told him that he was in the business of restoring old sewing machines that worked with foot pedals for power, vice electricity. He would also convert older electric models to foot operated models. He wanted to know if Risner could use the machines and asked for help in getting them to the Team. Major Risner quickly thought of the many war widows and orphans and came up with a plan. By working with local religious and civic leaders, needy widows would be identified as recipients of these machines. Risner made arrangements through the Third Marine Aircraft Wing, located at Marine Corps Air Station, El Toro, California to transport these machines to Vietnam. The logistics involved were not simple, especially since non-military cargo was involved, but it worked like a Swiss watch.

When the first three machines made their way to

Chu Lai and were uncrated all stared in awe at the craftsmanship involved. The wood finishes were spectacular, as if each wooden part had been hand rubbed with linseed oil producing a beautiful luster. The moving parts looked new and were painted with bright black enamel. The machines were lightly oiled and virtually noiseless in operation with a minimum of foot power. These sewing machines were works of art.

After consulting Pham and a local Buddhist priest, the first one was presented to a widow who lost her husband, an ARVN soldier, about one year previous. She was left with nine children and survived by hand-sewing clothes and by help from her neighbors. After she had been chosen, the local village chief and Buddhist priest accompanied the Team to her thatched hut. She had not been told anything beforehand and was visibly surprised and embarrassed at all the attention she was getting as she shyly came to the front of her hut. The machine was unloaded and placed it in front of her hut. She just stared at it as the village chief explained to her that it was hers. She shook her head from side to side, visibly distressed. Staff Sergeant Cong tried to explain. After a moment, Major Risner intervened and asked Staff Sergeant Cong, gently, what the problem was. Staff Sergeant Cong replied:

"She doesn't understand. She wants to know what is expected of her in return."

Major Risner: "Tell her Staff Sergeant Cong, that what we expect of her is nothing more than to love and support her children as she presently does and to accept this gift on behalf of a grateful Vietnam and America for the sacrifice her husband has made for all of us. She owes us nothing."

As Staff Sergeant Cong translated, she started crying and moved towards the machine with her children and she caressed it all over with her gnarled hands. She stood and addressed Major Risner and bowed with tears in her eyes and said,

"Cam On Ong," (Thank you).

Cong helped her place it in her hut where all of her neighbors oohed and awed and talked excitedly. There wasn't a dry eye among anyone. Commander Hartman sent a total of nine machines over a six month period. In every case the response was identical to that of the first recipient. The MAG-12 Civic Action Team was building a reputation of being a true and trusted friend to the people in all of the local villages and hamlets. It wasn't long before the Team found themselves inundated with requests. Major Risner tried to fill all of the requests according to the neediest.

Father Phuc, the Catholic Priest for the Dong Ha Orphanage, was one of those who received the most support on behalf of his needy parish. Unfortunately, the Father had needs, or should we say wants, that he tried to fill also from the generosity of the Team. Periodically Major Risner had to remind the Father whom he worked for and that personal gain would not curry favor with the Lord or Major Risner. With all the support he was already receiving from Rochester, the Father decided to go to another Marine outfit, MAG-13, and some of the other Army units requesting clothing also. After communicating with these other outfits and by doing a little investigative work, the Team found that the good Father was getting four or five times what he needed for the Orphanage and was having "yard sales" for the local populace. Although confident that the money was probably going to the Orphanage, Major Risner cut-off his other supply points and insisted they all coordinate with him before giving anything to the Orphanage. Later, it also came to the Team's attention that the good Father was selling pencils and paper tablets to the school children, supplies generously donated in large measure from Rochester, New York and in smaller measures from Iowa and California. The Team made an unannounced visit to the Catholic School one day to confirm this report. Not finding Father Phuc around, Major Risner asked one of the Nuns to show him where the school supplies donated by the Team were being stored. Upon opening the storage door, Major Risner was surprised to find out that the good Father was apparently operating his own brewery judging by the number of bottles of beer found. Later, Father Phuc insisted it was all a misunderstanding as he was only storing it for a friend. But from then on the Team made periodic unannounced visits and never had any other complaints or finds of misconduct. The Father once told Major Risner when he visited later that when he now made requests for supplies that his "other sources" had all referred him to Major Risner!

Partly because of his separation from his family in Saigon and partly because the Civic Action Team needed educational materials, Staff Sergeant Cong managed to get home every 30 to 60 days, compliments of Major Risner. Risner seldom failed to accomplish what he set out to do. On the first trip, he managed to get a set of travel orders for himself and Staff Sergeant Cong to go to Saigon on "Official Business". Major Risner used Cong as both interpreter and guide and found his way to the Ministry of Education in Saigon. Even though a Marine Major is a Field Grade Officer, Majors at that time in Vietnam were almost as plentiful as Second Lieutenants today. However, Major Risner managed an appointment with the Minister of Education for South Vietnam using General Walt's name by way of introduction. He deftly explained the problems in Chu Lai obtaining textbooks for the school children. What he didn't explain was his own knowledge that the cause of the problem was the graft and corruption (by Americans and Vietnamese alike) that resulted in only one out of every four or five children receiving a textbook. By the time everyone got their cut, there were hardly any left over. Whether admiring his chutzpa or intentions or due to his relationship with General Walt, from that time on any member of the Team had only to identify themselves by unit and a letter signed by Major Risner and the Team member was given the educational supplies. By using a contact with one of his buddies who was an Air Force Major in Da Nang with 20th Air Force Tactical Air Support Squadron (TASS), these supplies were normally flown home to Chu Lai in an Air Force spotter aircraft similar to the Marine Corps OV-10 Bronco.

The MAG-12 Civic Action reports sent to the 1st Marine Aircraft Wing in Da Nang generally detailed what, if any, materials or assistance was provided the local populace. For example, the Team would bring a Navy Corpsman into the villages to sanitize wells, provide instruction for proper personal hygiene and preventive medicine. Bars of soap, toothbrushes and toothpaste (something that many did not know of), and water purification tablets were handed out and the Corpsmen and Doctors who accompanied the Team would set-up temporary medical clinics whenever and wherever possible. They tried to explain the hazards of bathing directly around the wells and the Team provided cement for them to encircle the wells to prevent this. Through agencies like CARE and USAID (United States Agency for International Development) and local units like the Seabees and Army and Navy supply outfits the Team would provide building materials like wood and cement to build new schools or to add on to existing ones. Through generous support from countless people and local agencies or churches in the States, the Team was able to distribute school supplies and books for the schools as well as clothing and food for the orphanages that were rapidly expanding. English classes were held for the young and old. Instruction was provided on how to secure villages after dark and the Team worked with the CAP units who were living in many of these remote villages helping to provide defense. The Team helped to provide building materials for new temples and churches and attended the dedications and worked with youth organizations like the Buddhist Boy and Girl Scouts. While accomplishing these tasks the Team was always collecting intelligence whenever possible. This information was passed on to MAG-12 Group Intelligence and Americal Division Intelligence.

An equally important task was to assist in uniting these local people with their governments. They had no radio or television in I Corps except for AFVN (Armed Forces Vietnam Network). There was one television in the local village of An Tan, provided by the MAG-12 Civic Action Team, placed outside of the village headquarters where it was turned on and watched by many every night around 6:00pm. AFVN Da Nang would broadcast a half-hour news show followed by a half-hour Vietnamese soap opera all broadcast in the Vietnamese language. Other than their local governments and American soldiers, the villagers had no contact with the outside world. Some would have radios that could pick up short-wave and AM radio stations, but the majority did not. Through the Team's one to one contacts, people to people, the Team tried to spread the hope of a war being won in which they would have freedom and peace, two words almost forgotten in their vocabularies. Movies were shown in public areas by Army PYSOPS (Psychology Operations) providing all the right propaganda meant to unite a people with their government. But it was the one on one interaction, seeing and talking to an American soldier who treated them with respect and kindness that made the lasting impression. Vietnamese workers on the base were supplying intelligence

81

information without being asked. One worker told of a suspected Viet Cong rocket staged adjacent to a rice paddy close to the Group Guard perimeter. It turned out to be a spent JATO (Jet Assisted Take Off) bottle but the worker was rewarded with paid time off. Some in MAG-12s area actually came to believe that the Americans could end the war and establish a lasting democracy. But the majority expressed the feeling and hope that the war would end regardless of who won. Many would later say that these people didn't care about the War or the Americans trying to help them. When the Team would walk into a village, they would only see old men or young children. As often as not, they would find pictures of the missing family members inside the huts placed on a mantle containing a Buddhist memorial or on a table to remind all they were missed. In conversations with them, members of the Team were told many stories of young men going off to war and never being heard of again, or returning as amputees. Entire villages and families had been relocated as their homes were bombed or burnt. Village Chiefs were murdered wholesale at night unless they gave aid and comfort to the enemy. Wives and daughters were raped and beaten by both sides. Children were starved to death or died from diseases they were not inoculated against. Yes, they did give a damn and they placed the same value on life that Americans do.

TET OFFENSIVE 1968

On the Chinese Lunar New Year, January 31, 1968, North Vietnam launched the Tet Offensive. Every major US base in South Vietnam was attacked. Chu Lai, which had been exempt from attack since April of 1967, joined a long list of other seemingly safe havens like Cam Ranh Bay and Dalat that were attacked that night. Corporal Hays had finished some Civic Action reports and was sitting on his rack taking his clothes off when TAPS sounded. Lights were extinguished and he was counting z's by the time his head hit the pillow.

About ten minutes later he awoke to the sound of sirens going off and immediately thought it was another late night drill for the Reactionary Platoons. The Group Guard consisted of Marines from all of the Marine units assigned to Chu Lai regardless of their job specialty. They were deployed in 12 hour shifts 24/7 around the perimeter. The Reactionary Platoons were composed of all the other Marines not required to keep the aircraft up and running with ordnance. The Reactionary Platoons were the backup to the Group Guard. If the enemy broke through the perimeter the Reactionary Platoons were the last lines of defense. Quickly putting his clothes on and grabbing his rifle and 782 gear (cartridge belt, magazines, canteen, pack, etc) Hays ran out the hooch. He heard a couple of muffled booms from far away. His orders were to find the nearest bunker if any rockets or mortars were incoming otherwise he was to report immediately to the Command Bunker. All of the others not on duty on the flight line were to go to their assigned staging areas. On the way he didn't hear any additional booms just the confounded sound of the sirens.

Entering the Command Bunker Hays went to a desk with a topographical map of the area. Major Risner and Staff Sergeant Petterson were already in place, both on different field phones trying to get an overall picture of what was happening. On Hays' map, 6 watch towers strategically placed around the Air Base were marked with blue Xs. In addition to the map, the desk had a field phone resting on it, a PRC-25 field radio as well as a T-square and drafting compass. Spotters in the towers would call in through the Command Bunker switchboard where their calls were relayed to Hays. Each tower also had a radio in case the field phones did not function. From the information provided, Corporal Hays would try to triangulate the positions from where the rockets and/or mortars were launched; then he would pass on the map coordinates to Americal Division Fire Control Headquarters. From there the information was directed to the appropriate artillery unit or an air strike would be ordered. Air strikes could only be used if the aircraft were already in the air or if the airfield was not under attack. Charley knew this and would sometimes wait after the initial shelling until they saw activity on the flight line. Then they would direct rocket and/or mortar fire at the aircraft from a different location so as to avoid detection.

Artillery fire was not that effective because during the time it took to target the rockets or mortars the enemy would move to a different location. The Pacification program had greatly reduced the enemy's capacity to stash weapons but some of these had been stored in caches over two or three years previously. Hays' phone rang.

"Corporal Hays speaking, Sir." Then there was a long pause with Hays listening intently. "Good job Lance Corporal." Hays hung the phone up and turned in the direction of Major Risner who was now standing in front of a large wall map.

"Major Risner, Sir!" Hays barked out.

"What is it Corporal?"

"Sir, Zulu 3 reports three incoming rounds believed to be mortars fired from approximately 1000 meters out. No visible presence or incoming since then. No reports of damage, Sir." Zulu 3 was the tower overlooking the South end of the air strip where the bomb dump was located.

"Thank you Corporal Hays. Check the other towers and the Group Guard for activity."

"Aye, Aye, Sir!"

Corporal Hays reached for the handset of his PRC-25 radio. The radio was used when necessary to communicate with all of the towers, the Group Guard and other ground units simultaneously and as a back-up to the field phones.

"Team Zulu, Team Zulu this is Zulu Headquarters. Request sit rep, over"

Each tower responded by their number assigned.

"Zulu HQ, Zulu 1 negative report. Standing by, over." Negative report meant no activity had been spotted. Tower 2 responded the same. "Zulu HQ, Zulu 3 reports no change to previous sit rep. Standing by, over." Towers 4, 5 & 6 all had negative reports.

Corporal Hays again on the radio: "Team Golf, Team Golf, this is Golf Headquarters. Request sit rep, over." There were 4 reporting stations for the Group Guard equally divided between the North and South perimeters. Each of the 4 stations had negative reports

"Major Risner, Sir. All Golf and Zulu stations have negative reports."

"Thank you Corporal Hays. Send runners to the Reactionary Platoon Commanders and inform them of the present situation."

"Aye, aye, Sir!"

Risner said quietly to Petterson: "I don't like it. We expect some major action due to TET but I don't think this is it."

Petterson: "I agree, Sir. I think we ought to wait it out."

Risner nodded his head in agreement.

At the same time, all of the Reactionary Platoons from MAG-12 quickly formed in the designated area in Officers' Country and muster was taken. The Reactionary Platoons from MAG-13 were split between the North and South perimeters and were merged with the Group Guard positions. Each of the MAG-12 platoons was quickly dispersed to their foxholes. Extra ammo and grenades were passed out to everyone and they were being told that this was the real thing. Initial reports were that mortars were launched at the flight line from the southern perimeter and that the Group Guard was engaged and that the platoon should be prepared for a ground attack as this was normally preceded by such an event. This was clearly a departure from the norm. The base had not been hit since April of 1967 so there were a lot of Marines who had reported in since that last attack and they had never been through this before except in drills. After about ten minutes, the sirens quit and there was eerie silence all around as no one was allowed to talk possibly giving away their position. The word was passed to lock and load weapons. Designated personnel were given M-79 Grenade Launchers and M-60 Machine Guns were set-up. The Marines could see flares popping up around the perimeter every once in a while but they couldn't tell if these were trip flares or flares launched by the Group Guard. There was sporadic gunfire fueling the feeling that the base was going to be attacked by ground but no evidence of an all out firefight. If Charley got through the wire through the Group Guard line, the Reactionary Platoons were only about 200 meters behind them. There wasn't anything behind the platoons but the ocean.

Marine Staff Non-Commissioned Officers moved about quietly trying to calm and reassure everyone that they would all do well if the shit hit the fan. There was a lot of nervous tension for the next twenty minutes until the runner arrived from the Command Bunker and relayed the information from Major Risner to the Platoon leaders. Word was passed from one foxhole to the next that it was not an all out attack, just some harassment. Armorers went around and collected the extra rounds of ammo and the hand grenades. Within another 30 minutes another runner arrived from the Command Bunker with orders that when the all clear siren was heard, the platoon could be dismissed. When the siren at last went off, the platoon formed together and was dismissed.

Back in the Command Bunker, Risner said to Hays "Corporal Hays, you and the others here go get some shut-eye. Staff Sergeant Petterson will send a runner for you if needed."

Hays paused for a moment as something inside was telling him to stay. "Sir, with your permission I would like to stay a little longer."

"As you wish, you can secure everyone else."

"Aye, Aye Sir."

Hays relieved the switchboard operator and 6 other radio operators and runners all from the Comm (Communications) section and returned to his desk. He didn't feel sleepy as his adrenalin was still pumping from the previous events.

Everything was quiet for the next 45 minutes then all Hell broke loose. It seemed that explosions were occurring one right after the other all over the place. There were the thuds of mortars landing and exploding mixed with the crack and loud explosions of rockets. The sirens went off again, but this time no one was trying to get to the assembly area because the ground was shaking and it seemed as if the base was getting bombed. The field phones and radios came to life in the Command Bunker. Marines who worked the 12 hour day shifts raced from their racks to their individual bunkers adjacent to their hooches. Six feet underground and reinforced with sand bags on top and around the sides made it somewhat safe but as others found out that night if it took a direct hit the shrapnel might not get you but the concussion would. The shelling was continuous and went on for over an hour. It was a helpless feeling because no one knew exactly what was going on and there wasn't anyone to shoot at.

The rockets were being fired from a maximum range from several points due west and no one could do anything about it. Aircraft returning from missions were diverted to offshore carriers as the airfields at Da Nang and Chu Lai were closed. On the flight line everyone hunkered down in their above ground bunkers. Based on intelligence gathered by Major Risner beforehand, the Air Base Commander, Marine Col Julian White made a wise decision to move the A-6's belonging to VMA(AW)-533 to Ubon, Thailand. These aircraft were worth over $30 million a copy as compared to the $4 or $5 million cost of the F-4 Phantom. One of the A-6s was left behind, as it was a hanger queen (not operational due to a parts backlog, engine overhaul, or had been cannibalized for parts). That A-6 was destroyed by a direct hit to the hangar. This was the only hangar on the MAG-12 side of the flight line. All the other aircraft were parked in revetments (two-sided corrugated tin reinforced by sandbags on the tops of the side walls). The avionics complex consisted of a wooden building in the center of about 40 mobile maintenance vans. All of the lights had been turned off from the first moment of the attack. Generators were not cut off due to power requirements for the measurement standards that took 24 hours to recalibrate if the power was cut. These vans were like mini-trailers equipped with air conditioning and 400-cycle power needed for the systems maintained. Because this complex was located on the flight line, there were no below ground bunkers but instead had a couple of above ground bunkers heavily reinforced with Martian matting and sandbags. They would not survive a direct hit.

Some of the rockets found the runways creating large craters where they hit. Shrapnel was flung out in a wide arc slicing through anything in its path. 1st Lieutenant Francisco Alvarez (Frank to his friends) from Fort Worth Texas was situated in a make-shift fighting hole located at the top right corner on top of a revetment next to MAG-12's large Avionics Van Complex. He held a pair of binoculars in his hands looking out over the runway and beyond to the perimeter of the base. He was located about 100 meters west of the runway. Beyond the runway going east was another kilometer of land mostly used as a land fill and for one of the Army's Medical facilities, the 27th Surgical Hospital. Beyond that it was another kilometer east to the base perimeter and Highway 1 running north and south.

Any sappers or suicide squads would not want to approach the runways or aircraft from that direction as they would be easily spotted from one of the towers and/or aircraft and helicopter patrols. Just the same, Lieutenant Alvarez was going to make sure that anyone that did try to come in from that direction would not escape detection. Below him in the above ground bunkers were around 300 Marines between MAG-12 and MAG-13 armed and ready to protect the eastern side of the flight line if necessary.

On the southern end and east of the runway was the bomb dump. South of that by 2 kilometers was the group guard line and southern perimeter of the base. Captain Neil Millican from Durham North Carolina was the Officer in Charge of the Group Guard line. His primary Military Occupational Specialty was that of a Radar Intercept Officer in F-4B Phantoms. The flight surgeon had grounded him for 30 days due to a sinus and ear infection. His lack of experience as an Infantry Officer would not hamper his assignment as the gun emplacements, fields of fire and rules of engagement had been developed and implemented by Major Risner. Ever watchful during the initial attack, there was no evidence of a ground attack looming much to the displeasure of a few of the 120 Marines defending the southern perimeter and relief to most of the others. What they weren't expecting near the end of the attack was a direct hit on the bomb dump. Immediately these Marines realized what had happened while the rest of the base didn't know. It was an ear-deafening explosion causing the sandbagged walls inside of each bunker to actually vibrate up and down about six inches. Everyone thought that the enemy had either hit the fuel farm just South of the MAG-12 living area on the beach or the base was being bombed. When the shelling stopped, Charley was probably happy with the damage they inflicted. As to whether they had known that most of the A-6s had been removed will never be known. The base had taken over 150 incoming rockets most aimed at the flight line. Parts of runways were lost and several hangars and aircraft were damaged. Strays had found some bunkers and other buildings in living areas causing casualties, as well as the fuel farm. Fortunately, Charley did not hit any of the above ground fuel storage tanks. There was a tanker offshore that was transferring fuel and there had been no time to transfer all the above ground fuel to below ground.

During the shelling, Captain Millican sent runners from his Command Position bunker to the two far ends of his guard line and told them to work their way back towards the middle. The message was brief: "As soon as the shelling stops be ready for a ground attack. Make sure all of your weapons are locked and loaded."

For five minutes after the shelling stopped there was a dead silence except for the occasional explosion from the bomb dump. From the western end of the guard line a trip flare went off, followed by another closer to the middle. The bright light illuminated the night unveiling 10 Viet Cong in black pajamas and coolie hats with charges strapped to the front and backs of their bodies trying to climb over the concertina wire on the perimeter. One of the three fifty caliber machine guns opened fire followed by a second in the middle. One of the heads exploded. Another body was cut in half at the waist. The Viet Cong coming in behind him took a round in his left shoulder and then his body seemed to disintegrate as the next round hit the explosive charges bound to his chest. All of a sudden the perimeter lights controlled by Americal Division Ground Defense Headquarters came on exposing all of the Marines' defensive positions. With the Marines exposed, enemy mortar positions zeroed in quickly and began laying down a barrage. At the same time whistles were blowing and hard core NVA troops began charging the lines behind the Viet Cong. Captain Millican was immediately on the radio requesting the lights be turned off. Major Risner in turn radioed Americal Division requesting then demanding the lights be turned off.

"You're exposing my men's positions! Turn them damn lights off or my men will shoot them out!"

The lights were out in 30 seconds but the damage had been done. One of the 50 caliber machine guns was taken out by an enemy mortar and three of the gun crew were killed. The North Vietnamese Army charge was short lived as the remaining gun emplacements literally mowed the enemy soldiers downed. As Captain Millican ordered his troops to stand down, one last mortar found its mark. He was 29 years young, father of two girls aged 3 and 5, husband to the former Nancy McGregory of Petaluma, CA.

The next day, a squad from the Group Guard found the bodies of over a dozen Viet Cong and close to 30 North Vietnamese Army soldiers. Most didn't look much older than 16. Many had marijuana cigarettes half-smoked attached to their hatbands. One of the officers had a red MAO book in his shirt pocket.

For all the damage, the Seabees had the runway operational again within twenty-four hours. The base began a round-the-clock 72-hour clean-up operation that restored nearly everything to operational. The Army-Navy-Marine Corps Team functioned superbly. If Charley had thought he was going to intimidate or demoralize the troops, it had the opposite effect. Individual efforts of bravery and valor were common and many were cited. Everyone had a sense of pride and determination that was always there, but now was being exhibited openly and unabashedly. The base, the Army and the Marine Corps had been tested and each passed with flying colors. Nerves were still on edge as the bomb dump continued to "cook" for about two days later creating intermittent explosions, until the decision was made to have an aircraft drop a 1000 pound bomb in the middle ending the explosions. The word was passed around so everyone would know what was going on. For three days the Air Base had regrouped and become fully operational again.

AMBUSH!

On a warm day in April of 1968, the Marine Aircraft Group 13 Civic Action Officer came to see Major Risner. He was going on R&R to Hawaii in a week and asked Major Risner if he would cover for him during his absence. The only thing scheduled, was the dedication of a new Buddhist Temple recently constructed in the village of Long Phu II. The date was set a few days earlier and they were expected to attend. MAG-13's Civic Action Tactical Area of Responsibility covered an area behind An Tan and 9th Engineers, about three miles from the base in the direction of the mountains. The MAG-12 Team had been in this area just a couple of times to assist MAG-13 on their request. Since MAG-13's area was relatively small, the Civic Action Officer didn't have a Staff Non-Commissioned Officer assigned to him permanently. His staff was made up of volunteers from the squadrons as a collateral duty. The Major told him that he would be glad to assist and the date was recorded on the "To Do" list for April 26, 1968 for early afternoon. Major Risner, Staff Sergeant Petterson, Staff Sergeant Cong and Corporal Hays would attend. The next day, Major Risner and the afore mentioned members went out to the temple while it was still under construction to be sure of its location. Everything looked to be on schedule and some of the villagers waved as the Team went by.

When the day came for the dedication of the

temple, Staff Sergeant Cong and Corporal Hays were scheduled to attend to some business in Ky Khoung that morning. They would be back by 1300 hours (1:00pm) to leave for Long Phu II. It was either a mistake in scheduling or the time was changed, because when Cong and Hays returned on time, they were told that the Major and Petterson had already left.

Corporal Hays said to Staff Sergeant Cong, "I don't think they needed us, or they wouldn't have left without us. I wish that we hadn't missed them and the dedication of the temple but it's no big deal."

Staff Sergeant Cong replied, "I think I should have gone with them. They are probably mad at me now."

"If the Major and Dick were really concerned about it, they would have waited for us. So don't be upset or jump to conclusions."

To his credit, Staff Sergeant Cong had a tremendous sense of duty and unquestionable loyalty to the Major.

By 1600 (4:00pm), the remainder of the Team was wondering what was taking the Major and Dick so long, when they heard a commotion outside the office and the sound of a jeep pulling up. Everyone stared in amazement at the jeep and the two occupants. The jeep was bullet-ridden with many holes through the windshield and a visibly exhausted pair of Marines. The Major had a tear in the left sleeve of his jungle utilities where blood was still trickling and both the Major and Dick had tears on their uniforms and scrapes with a little blood here and there. They had yet to receive any medical attention and it was clear the adrenaline was still pumping as the Team got bits and pieces of what happened. Many officers and enlisted personnel gathered around as word spread throughout the group compound. The "official" story as it appeared in Stars and Stripes under the heading "Two Marines Bust VC Trap":

"CHU LAI (USMC) - Marine Aircraft Group (MAG)-12 civil affairs teams have worked in the villages and hamlets around Chu Lai for more than two years without any major incidents with the Viet Cong. When trouble did arrive, it came in a grenade-flinging firefight with a Viet Cong ambush unit. The recent incident took place three miles west of Chu Lai, when Major Richard F. Risner, MAG-12 civil affairs officer, and Staff Sergeant Richard M. Petterson headed their jeep over the last hill entering the valley near Long Phu II village. The VC had set up an "L" shaped ambush on the road. A burst of gunfire through the windshield missed both Marines. However, both received superficial wounds from flying glass. Major Risner and Sgt. Petterson rolled out on the ground and using the jeep for cover, commenced firing at the rifle muzzle flashes in the bush that concealed the members of the Viet Cong ambush. Suddenly, a grenade landed beside the Major! "I saw it, grabbed it, and threw it back," he said. "Another grenade landed some 15 feet away and gave Sgt. Petterson a good jolt." The volume of fire from the two .45 caliber pistols and the M-16 rifle carried by Major Risner and Sgt. Petterson were sufficient to discourage the Viet Cong ambushers who withdrew into the bush leaving two slightly wounded Marines who consider themselves extremely lucky to be alive."

Both the Major and Petterson were taken to the dispensary where their wounds were treated and they returned for a debriefing by S-2 (Intelligence). The next day Major Risner told the team what had happened.

"We had our times mixed up. We were supposed to be there at 1300 which meant we needed to leave at least an hour and a half before that."

They had left in a new jeep, an M-151 and for whatever reason the canvas covering the top, rear and sides was in place. Dick had decided to take along one of the M-16's the Group Guard had in the armory as well as his regulation side arm, a 45 caliber pistol. He had 200 rounds of ammo for the rifle and 2 magazines of ammo for his pistol. Major Risner carried his 45 caliber pistol as well in a brand new leather holster he got at the Armory. As was the regular routine they were not wearing combat helmets or flak jackets.

Risner told the other members of the Team, "We were rounding a curve going up the hill with Dick driving and I was riding shotgun. Petterson drove to the top of a hill slowing to 2 or 3 mph and was leaning out the side of the jeep to try to check the downgrade when the windshield exploded. With no time to say anything Dick bailed out the left side and I bailed out on the right. I felt pain in my left shoulder but I figured it was a piece of glass from the windshield."

Petterson: "As I bailed out I remembered the M-16 lying between the seats and I grabbed it with my right hand. As the bursts continued the jeep rolled slightly forward and died giving us some protection. I began to fire in the direction of the muzzle flashes with my M-16."

Risner: "I shouted to Dick that I could not get my 45 out of my holster. It was a new holster and the leather flap was about a quarter of an inch thick. I was unable to loosen the snap and I was trying everything to get the pistol out. By the time Dick tossed his 45 to me I somehow got the other pistol out and I was using them both."

Petterson was smiling, "Can you believe it? Here we were in a skirmish for our lives and I see the Major with pistols working in both hands. All I could think of was how he reminded me of John Wayne, left and right guns blazing and I had to laugh out loud! The enemy must have heard it and thought I was crazy as they stopped shooting for just a moment."

At this point the Major produced the new holster with the bottom of the flap still buttoned and the top half ripped in two. In the heat of the moment with the adrenaline pumping, Major Risner had ripped the top off the holster!

Petterson: "It (silence) didn't last for long. A grenade was tossed towards us and rolled towards the Major. He didn't hesitate. The Major picked it up and tossed it back!" Risner: "Just after that, another grenade rolled towards us and there was nothing we could do except make ourselves as small a target as possible. The grenade went off closer to Dick than me and I was concerned that he had been killed or wounded badly by the shrapnel. It was right after this that three of our attackers emerged from the thicket in front of us screaming and yelling with bayonets fixed. I aimed my pistols at the one closest to my flank and I saw him go down. By the time I turned my aim on the other two, I saw Dick out of the corner of my eye stand up and fire a burst into the other two killing them instantly."

Petterson: "I could tell from their uniforms that they weren't the regular NVA or VC. They were wearing the camouflage of the VC Tiger Guerillas."

Risner: "I don't know if there were others involved and we didn't hang around to find out. We got back into the jeep and came home."

Petterson: "Kind of surprised the Americal Division MPs when we came through the main gate." Smiling, Petterson continued: "I told them we had just saved them from the attack of a NVA Division. Can you believe the guy gave me the finger?"

Everyone laughed at that. As word of the attack made rounds through the base and out in the villages Pham told Major Risner that there were prices on the heads of the Civic Action Team. "You are winning the people over and your name has spread throughout our area. The people are rejecting the lies of the VC and they are denying them sanctuary and refusing to hide their arms and supply goods. They are turning them over to the PFs and CAP units."

Risner smiling: "Nice to know we are appreciated."

Pham: "No joke, Thieu ta. Word is you have price of $500.00 American on your head alone. This from General Giap's Headquarters."

General Giap was the overall NVA Commander.

Risner still smiling: "How would General Giap know me?"

Pham: "He see your picture in <u>Stars and Stripes</u> like everyone else. You think only Americans read that propaganda? Ask Nguyen in Ky Khoung, he will tell you the same."

Now Risner wasn't smiling. "I'm just one of thousands of American Officers. It's flattering but I don't think I am that important."

Pham shrugged his shoulders in resignation. He added: "You be extra careful Major."

For his actions involving bravery and heroism in throwing back the grenade and successfully driving off their attackers, Major Risner was awarded the Silver Star with Combat "V" for Valor. For his actions involving bravery and heroism in repelling their attackers, Staff Sergeant Petterson was awarded the Bronze Star with Combat "V" for Valor. For wounds sustained in combat as a result of engaging the enemy, both were awarded the Purple Heart. As further recognition of his leadership and presence of mind in a combat situation, Staff Sergeant Petterson received a combat promotion to Gunnery Sergeant. To Petterson, the promotion was better than the award.

Chau Tu

The trips to the Quaker Rehabilitation Center in Quang Ngai increased in frequency and number immediately following the TET Offensive. Unfortunately, one of the female doctors had left on vacation two days prior to TET to meet up with another female colleague in Hue City and both became prisoners of war. They were not released until May of 1968. Because of the destruction and havoc, the hospital in Quang Ngai didn't operate during this time so there was quite a backlog by May.

As word spread that the Marines in Chu Lai would transport victims for free, many who had become amputees as far back as the Second World War and the War of Independence with France came seeking help. No one was turned away even though the Marines often paid for victim's meals, clothing and even medicine. Donations were made and accepted by the Quakers from the Marines and other Army units and soldiers. Because children grow at a faster rate, multiple trips were needed and Corporal Hays took the lead in making sure that follow-up visits were made as required.

During one such trip, Corporal Hays was transporting Pham Luec, an 8 year old boy who lost his left leg below the knee due to mortar shrapnel. Pham Luec had already been to Rehabilitation Center in November of 1967 where he was fitted with his first prosthetic leg. By May of 1968 he was ready for a new prosthetic leg to adjust for his growth. Although it wasn't prudent, Corporal Hays made the trip by himself as the other Team members were engaged elsewhere in the ever-expanding realm of responsibility and he knew Pham was overdue for an adjustment.

Arriving at the Center in Quang Ngai in the early morning without incident, Corporal Hays left Pham Luec with one of the nurses until the doctor was ready for him. Hays went to one of the village vendors operating a push-cart and ordered a bowl of Chinese noodles with some type of meat that he didn't care to question along with a warm Coca-Cola. Finding an empty stool under a large tarp covering the cart, he began to eat enjoying the shade of a hot afternoon.

He looked up to see a Vietnamese Popular Forces soldier riding a motorcycle too fast through the narrow streets up to the entrance of the Clinic where he hit the brakes in a cloud of dust before plowing through the door. Thinking of Pham Luec, Hays dropped his bowl, reached for his 45 pistol and began to run towards the Clinic. By the time he reached the PF soldier, several people from the Clinic came out to see what the commotion was. The soldier was talking in a loud voice with animated gestures and a crowd of onlookers began to gather around him. Hays caught the words Chau Tu and recognized the name of the village. Chau Tu was a refugee hamlet, which by definition meant that it was a gathering of war refugees from the surrounding area who found themselves homeless due to their villages being destroyed either by the Viet Cong or American Forces. Hays passed the village of Binh

103

Son about 5 kilometers from Quang Ngai on Highway One and Chau Tu was about 1 ½ kilometers east of Binh Son.

When at last the soldier had finished talking to the workers in the clinic, Hays cornered one of the female doctors and asked what the soldier was saying.

"He said that late last night and into the early morning, a battle was fought between NVA and U.S. Army soldiers close to Chau Tu. While the fighting was going on, Viet Cong forces came to Chau Tu and burned the village to the ground. Before burning the entire village, the VC captured the Village Chief, his wife and two children, both young boys less than 5 years old. The VC forced the entire village to witness their deaths."

The doctor lost her composure for a moment, then with tears in her eyes continued.

"Before they executed the family, the VC told the other villagers that they were being taught a lesson as to what happens when they aid the Americans. Then one of the VC took the youngest boy who was crying, grabbed him upside down by the ankles and threw his head in a wide arc over the soldier's head onto a large rock on the ground, smashing his head like a watermelon."

She stopped speaking again, now visibly sobbing.

"That's okay," Hays said. "I get the idea."

"No, there is more," she composed herself again. "You need to hear this; you need to know what happens when you come to another country interfering in matters that don't concern you."

"I'm sorry," Corporal Hays offered, "But I am not the one that made that decision nor do I take responsibility for atrocities committed by the other side."

"We see them from both sides," the doctor retorted.

Hays said nothing.

The doctor continued, "The other boy was made to bend over at the waist while another of the VC soldiers beheaded him with a machete. Next, the mother was laid out, spread-eagled, while she was repeatedly beaten and raped by six VC soldiers. While this was going on, the Village Chief, her husband and father of the two boys, was placed in a sitting position and disemboweled. He watched the spectacle while witnessing his own entrails slowly leaving his body. Both were thrown barely alive into a bonfire along with the boys."

Corporal Hays paused for a moment, looked the doctor in the eyes and asked if he could leave Pham Luec at the clinic for the rest of the day and possibly the night. He explained that he was not abandoning Pham and that he would speak to him and reassure him that he would take him home by tomorrow at the latest.

"What will you do?" the doctor asked, realizing that Hays was going to the burned down hamlet.

"Whatever I can," Hays replied.

After spending a full ten minutes explaining to Pham that he would definitely return to take him home, Hays set out for Chau Tu.

Arriving in Binh Son, there was no indication that a major battle had just occurred near Chau Tu. The village hummed with the normal activity, merchants and markets were busy hawking their wares and there was no sign of any military presence except for an occasional soldier picking up his laundry or driving through the village on business. Corporal Hays decided to stop one of the soldiers standing in front of Linda's Laundry.

"How's it hanging, Sergeant?" Hays asked in a friendly manner.

"Low," he answered smiling.

"At least it's there and hanging," Hays replied.

"No shit. What's the Marine Corps doing here?" the Sergeant asked.

"Dropped off a patient in Quang Ngai. I heard there was some shit going on near Chau Tu. Hear anything about that?"

"Yeah, some of the guys from the 11th Infantry Brigade ran into some NVA troops last night. I heard some of the radio chatter from our Comm section."

"Hear anything about Chau Tu, itself?" Hays asked.

"No, was something going on there? I know one of the bar girls from there."

"I heard in Quang Ngai that the place was torched."

"No shit? I hope Cookie is okay. Are you headed that way?"

"Yeah," Hays replied, "But I haven't been there before."

"Hell, I'll go with you. I don't have to be back to my unit till dark. My name's Oze, but you can call me Turk."

"Okay, Sergeant Turk," Hays said smiling. "My name is Corporal Gene Hays."

"Drop the Sergeant bullshit and just call me Turk." Turk reached out his hand to shake, "Glad to meet you Jarhead, I mean Gene."

"Likewise, and smile when you say Jarhead," Hays replied.

Turk jumped into the jeep with Hays and gave him directions out of Binh Son towards the village of Chau Tu. Turk explained it was only a couple of kilometers away as they passed over some small hills on a narrow road, shared by ox carts, water buffalo and people alike.

"It's just over this next hill," Turk pointed ahead.

As they came over a hill and down into a valley, Hays could see some wisps of smoke emanating from the center of what used to be a village. Stopping the jeep to take in the view below, both Hays and Turk got out of the jeep.

Looking incredulous, Turk exclaimed, "I don't fucking believe it! There's nothing left! There must have been at least 200 people living here and all of their huts are gone, their livestock, everything. I wonder where the people are?"

Hays pointed to a small area dotted with trees atop the next hill and about 200 meters behind where the village used to exist. "I'll bet what's left is there. Let's go!"

When Hays and Turk reached the crest of the hill, they saw what was left of the population of Chau Tu. Corporal Hays began to ask in Vietnamese if anyone spoke English. Turk went to look for his friend Cookie but was told she left to go to Quang Ngai to an Aunt's house. He was pointed to one of the elders who was crouched in the traditional manner, holding his head in his hands, moaning all the while.

"Chao, Thua Ong," Corporal Hays said to the man, holding his hands together in front while bowing. In Vietnamese Hays asked the Elder if he spoke English. He nodded his head yes. After asking what happened to the village, the Elder told Hays the same story he had heard in Quang Ngai. What had been left out was the part about the execution of all the males between 10 and 50 years old. These unlucky few who were unfit for military service, usually for mental or physical defects were shot in the head; some were shot trying to run, others were killed trying to protect their families. That left the women and girls, some of whom had been raped, beaten and killed by the VC. The message was clear: to help the Americans meant death. Of the over 200 members of the Chau Tu Refugee Hamlet, only half that number survived and they had lost everything.

After hearing the old man's story, Hays asked Turk if he thought his Army unit could help. Turk replied that between the two of them they might be able to do so.

"What have you got in mind?" Turk asked.

"We need tents, shelter halves, basic tools and

utensils, clothing and food," Hays answered.

"How are going to get all of that? We don't have clothes for the kids and the women," Turk replied. "I don't think the Quartermaster (Supply) will just give us any of that stuff for civilians."

"They're not just civilians, they are war casualties. We have some clothes in Chu Lai and other materials donated to us from the States. As for the food and other items, I may have something to barter with when we talk to your Quartermaster."

"The Quartermaster by definition has everything. What are you going to bribe him with, money?" Turk asked.

"Something money can't buy," Hays said smiling.

"What's that?" Turk asked again.

"War trophies," Hays replied. "Have you ever seen a captured NVA flag?"

For the next two weeks Corporal Hays and Sergeant Turk made return trips to Binh Son and Chu Lai trying to drum up support for their effort. At the first stop in Binh Son, Corporal Hays met the Quartermaster and told him what was needed. The Quartermaster agreed to collect all that he could on such a short notice with the caveat that the war trophy be delivered for inspection the next day. Hays agreed and also asked if Sergeant Turk could accompany him to Chu Lai and back and help him for the next few days. The Quartermaster called his best friend at the Army Medical Clinic and cinched the deal. He informed Sergeant Turk that he was now quarantined to the hospital for the next couple of weeks due to malaria.

When Hays and Turk returned the next day in the late afternoon in a 6 bye truck from Chu Lai, it was loaded with canned goods, eggs, bread and all kinds of produce and cases of C-Rations that included candy and cigarettes. Fresh meat wasn't practical or even possible due to the lack of refrigeration but there were cases of canned boned turkey and ham and lots of Spam. There were boxes of children's clothing, donated from the United States along with school supplies to get the school operating again. Marine Corps Supply provided cooking pots, utensils, canteens, blankets, sleeping bags, shelter halves and inflatable mattresses. Individual Marines donated candy, snacks, health and beauty aids all purchased with their own money from the Marine Exchange. When the truck arrived at Chau Tu, Hays and Turk were immediately surrounded by all of the villagers. Smiles abounded throughout the crowd while many cried and some were still mourning the loss of their loved ones. The shelter halves began to sprout up immediately as the women took the lead in setting up temporary shelters. Hays unhooked a Water Buffalo from his truck, loaded with 500 gallons of fresh water. Most of the villagers had no idea what it was until Hays opened one of the spigots and water came out. Many of the elderly came to Hays and Turk wanted to touch them and thank them for their generosity.

Around mid-day, having unloaded everything from the truck with the help of the locals, Hays and Turk were resting under a shade tree. Moments later, something kicked the dust up at their feet.

"What the Hell was that?" Hays said out loud.

"I don't know," Turk replied. "Maybe one of the kids threw a rock."

"From where?" Hays began when it happened once again.

"Shit!" Turk exclaimed. "Look to your right, about 300 meters out. Some asshole is shooting at us!"

Both Hays and Turk immediately went to the prone position. Hays yelled out to the rest of the villagers telling them to look for cover. Turk aimed his M-16 at the figure as did Hays with his M-14. Turk fired first.

"I think he's too far out for that M-16. Keep firing though while I zero in."

Turk squeezed off another round while Hays adjusted his weapon.

"One click up elevation, no wind adjustment," Hays said to himself and he squeezed off a round.

"Stop firing Turk. I think my round went short. I'll make an adjustment and wait a couple of minutes and maybe he'll show himself."

More than 5 minutes went by without any firing from both sides.

"I think he's a lone sniper or we would have a fire fight in the making," Hays said.

"I think you're right," replied Turk.

Another five minutes went by and the figure made the mistake of rising to his knees. Hays took a deep breath, closed one eye, and aimed for the 12 o'clock sight picture and squeezed off a round. The figure's head exploded.

"You got him!" Turk exclaimed.

Hays went back to the group of villagers to let them know that the immediate danger was over. A group of women retrieved the dead soldier's body, dragging it back into the village. He looked to be no more than 16 years old. As they passed by Hays and Turk, one of the elderly women stopped.

"He number ten VC!" she said pointing to the dead soldier. "He spy on us for the VC and cause us big trouble."

She then spat on the body as did the other women. They dragged the body around the small tent village where several people spat on or kicked the lifeless form. After everyone had a chance to see the dead body, it was taken to the outskirts and burned.

Near dusk, Hays and Turk returned to Binh Son and Hays went immediately to the Quartermaster.

"Okay," the Quartermaster said. "What have you got for me?"

Hays went back to the cab of his truck and returned with a rifle and handed it to the Army Sergeant First Class without a word.

The Quartermaster looked it over and gave it a quick visual inspection.

"Alright, so it's a Russian SKS. It's nice but I would have preferred an AK-47. Is that it?"

"Well, I do have something else but I have been saving it for an emergency," Hays replied.

"Out with it, Corporal, I've got things to do," the Sergeant demanded.

Hays got a doubtful look on his face as if

wondering what to do.

"I don't know. If I give this up it's worth a lot more than that SKS."

The Quartermaster looked at Hays, trying to decide what to do next. After a long silence, he said, "If it's any good, I'll match whatever your Marine Corps Supply provided, understanding though you have to pick it up from Americal Division in Chu Lai and deliver it yourself."

Hays allowed a small grin to form on his face as he reached inside his jungle utility jacket. "I hate to give this up but I guess it's worth it." He then pulled out a folded triangular cloth from under his breast pocket and held it in his hand looking at it intently.

"What the Hell is that?" the Quartermaster asked sarcastically.

Hays began to unfold the material revealing a red flag with a gold star in the middle. There was a bullet hole through the folds and evidence of blood stains throughout. As Hays began to speak the Quartermaster's eyes began to bulge.

"During the TET Offensive, a company sized North Vietnamese Army Unit charged one of our CAP outposts near Chu Lai. The NVA Commanding Officer and all of his 60 men were killed by automatic weapons fire in a matter of minutes. As the Commanding Officer fell to the ground he was observed by one of our Marine Gunners to be reaching inside his jacket. Fearing he was reaching for a satchel charge, the Marine drilled him through the chest with an M-14 round. When the battle was over, he went to the NVA

Major who still had his hand inside his jacket and found that he was clutching this flag that I hold now. Out of gratitude for the assistance we gave his CAP unit, the Marine who retrieved the flag gave it to my Civic Action Unit along with this Letter of Testimony, describing what I have just told you and signed by the Marine who shot the NVA Officer and retrieved the flag, Gunnery Sergeant R.M. Petterson, United States Marine Corps."

At first the Quartermaster was dumbfounded and could not speak. His eyes became moist as he reached out to take the flag.

"I will be forever grateful. I can't believe it. Thank you so much. I will treasure this always."

"No problem," Hays replied. "Do you still want the rifle?" Hays asked.

"No, I don't need the rifle but thanks anyway."

Sergeant Turk didn't know about the flag and looked visibly upset. After leaving the Quartermaster who was telling everyone he could about his good fortune, Hays took Turk aside.

"I lied about the flag," Hays said.

"What?" Turk asked.

"The NVA Major was really a Captain."

"And that's supposed to make me feel better?" Turk replied.

"No, but you can have the SKS rifle."

"Thanks," Turk said, "I appreciate it."

"No sweat," Hays said. "Do you want to hear the story behind this rifle?"

Over the next two weeks Corporal Hays and

Sergeant Turk made repeat trips back to Chau Tu bringing whatever supplies they could scrounge up. The Viet Cong never returned probably figuring they had done enough damage. Fighting continued sporadically through the area sometimes disrupting the visits by Hays and Turk. Occasionally a lone sniper would try to take a pot shot at the two but the people of Chau Tu kept them protected by surrounding them whenever they came into their village. The day Hays and Turk made their farewell, the new village of Chau Tu honored them with a meal and heartfelt thanks.

Khuong Quang

August 20th of 1968 was a typical sunny, humid and hot day in South Vietnam. Major Risner was down to less than a month before he was due to "rotate" or transfer back to the States. A couple of weeks before that date the Team had made one of their usual visits to Americal Division to get an update from intelligence. Analysis was made as to what villages were considered "hot" and which ones were considered pacified. One remaining area, Khoung Quang Village, about 10 kilometers northwest from the base was considered friendly by day and hostile at night.

By this time almost 90 percent of the area had been pacified exceeding even Major Risner's expectations. The Team had made remarkable progress (noted by the Army and Marine Corps) in converting some of these hot spots from either known enemy held or enemy occupied at night to friendly villages. The result was evidenced by reduced hostile activity in these areas, including using them as launching sites for rockets and/or mortars. Major Risner wanted Khoung Quang added to the friendly column.

The order of the day for the enemy was to launch rockets and mortars without being detected and occasionally to try suicide assaults against American fortifications. There were some sapper assaults where a handful would penetrate the base defenses and try to plant their charges amongst the aircraft, but these rarely succeeded. The major objective was to destroy as many aircraft as possible and cause as much mayhem as possible to demoralize the troops.

The Civic Action Team's mission was to go out to the hostile areas and try to connect with the people of the village and prevent these attacks. It was a slow and dangerous process for all involved. Civic Action Teams were trying to win the hearts and minds of the people while the enemy was trying to instill fear and subservience through murder and torture.

The next day after getting all the information on the location of Khoung Quang Village from Americal Division, the Team set out to contact the village chief. Major Risner, Gunnery Sergeant Petterson, Staff Sergeant Cong, Corporal Hays, Corporal McKillips and Private First Class Williams went in two vehicles out the main gate of the base, and then headed north along the main service road, Highway One. They traveled through the village of An Tan, across the bridge and just past the village of Ky Lien. The Army Advisory Unit at Ly Tin District headquarters was about one or two kilometers farther north. It was visible from where the vehicles were parked on the west side of the road by the railroad tracks. There were maybe a dozen bamboo huts around this area filled with local inhabitants. The people always waved at the Team whenever they went by.

From the point where the vehicles were parked, the Team had to hike towards the west for 2 or 3 kilometers because of the rice paddies and lack of road. As the Team made an entrance to the village, it caused a lot of excitement amongst the children as most of them had never seen an American. Everyone was armed but it was low key as always on one of these missions. Corporal Hays carried his 45 pistol, as did Major Risner and the interpreter Staff Sergeant Cong. Gunnery Sergeant Petterson had his Thompson 45 grease gun and the rest carried M-14 rifles. None were wearing combat helmets or flak jackets; just soft covers and no one was carrying any special hardware like grenades or automatic weapons. The Team met with the village chief and elders and drank hot tea while the Major conversed with them through the interpreter, Staff Sergeant Cong. The Team spent a good couple of hours with an amiable exchange of pleasantries and about what could be done to help the village. A date was set for 10 days away when the Team would return with the first gesture of help consisting of school supplies. They would bring paper, pencils, notebooks, crayons and the like. The Village leaders were very appreciative and all went well as the Team bade them goodbye in the traditional manner of hands clasped while bowing.

With the date set for the 20th of August, the Team forgot about the village until the day before when they accumulated all the supplies they were going to take. They had done this type of mission many times and they were looking forward to meeting the people again. Gunnery Sergeant Petterson had just returned from R & R in Hawaii and had decided to stay behind to unpack his gear. The morning the Team was to leave, the VMA(AW)-533 Civic Action Team Officer, Captain Greenwold, called and asked what was planned this day, as they had never been able to go out with the Team on a mission. Major Risner invited them to come along. It was a good idea as Captain Greenwold was slated to replace Major Risner when he went home. There had been five people scheduled to go on this mission but now there were eight extra members from 533. They were told not to bring helmets or flak jackets, just their normal weapons they were issued.

Everyone traveled in 5 vehicles back to the same area where the Team had parked their vehicles during the initial visit before hiking west to the village. Leaving the vehicles behind, the Team placed the school supplies under their arms and headed towards Khuong Quang; nothing seemed out of the ordinary. The main body of the group headed towards the village with Corporal McKillips and Corporal Hays bringing up the rear. The Team had hiked almost a kilometer up and down a couple of small hills when Major Risner was heard conversing with Captain Greenwold about something. They stopped and the Major headed back towards Corporal Hays.

"Corporal Hays, I forgot I was supposed to meet Major Nourse from the Ly Tin Advisory Team at the MSR where we parked our vehicles. I am going to go back to the MSR and see if he is there."

"Do you want me to go with you?" asked Hays.

"No, it's not necessary. I'll wait by my jeep until Major Nourse shows up. I don't want us to be late for our meeting and Major Nourse and I will join you within a few minutes."

As the group started to move on, Hays hailed

Captain Greenwold.

"I think Corporal McKillips and I should remain behind a few minutes until the two Majors return. Staff Sergeant Cong knows the way to the village."

Greenwold agreed and the rest of the Group continued on and out of sight. Hays and McKillips engaged in some small talk for the next 15 minutes. Hays began to be concerned when after another 15 minutes went by and no one showed up.

"Doug, you wait here while I go back and check on the two Majors."

Jogging at a medium pace, it only took Hays 10 minutes to get back to the road where he found all the vehicles still parked, but no sign of Major Risner or Major Nourse and no Army vehicle. Hays asked a couple of villagers, both old men, if they had seen an American Major. Hays: "Thieu ta Nguoi My o'dau?" (Where did the American Major go?)

Both shook their heads. "Khong biet," (Don't know.)

Hays then saw a young girl carrying water to a hut. He was surprised to see her as he recognized her as Phan Thi Lan, one of the students Major Risner had sponsored for a scholarship award.

"Phan, it's good to see you," Hays was thankful he had found someone that he knew.

"Have you seen Major Risner today?"

"I think I saw him get into the back of a truck."

Hays thought that the Major wouldn't hitchhike or jump into the back of any truck when he had a perfectly good jeep to drive. And where was Major

Nourse?

"Phan, I thought you lived in Ky Lien. Why are you here?"

"I come to visit my grandmother who is sick. I must go back to her know."

Hays watched as she quickly returned to the hut.

He immediately got in his vehicle and drove up the road to Ly Tin and the Army Advisory Unit. Much to his dismay he found Major Nourse alone. Hays told him what happened and Nourse told him he forgot about meeting Major Risner. Now Hays was very worried. He told Nourse he was going back to get the main group. Major Nourse said he and his unit would meet the Team by the parked vehicles.

Hays drove back to the other vehicles, jumped out and ran as fast as he could back to McKillips. Hays told him what happened and instructed him to quickly find the main group and meet him back at the vehicles. Hays then ran all the way back to the road and found Major Nourse and about a dozen Vietnamese Popular Forces fanned out canvassing all the huts in the area. The PFs reported that either the villagers had not seen the Major or had related different stories about seeing him leave with another American soldier or hitchhiking back to base. Now Hays was really concerned for Major Risner.   The main group finally made its way back to the road. It seemed like an hour but was probably half that. Again Major Nourse and Corporal Hays reiterated what they knew. Staff Sergeant Cong looked devastated. Captain Greenwold made the decision that the group would return to base, inform the command and then return for a full-fledged search. Major Nourse said he would leave some of his men where the Major disappeared, return to Ly Tin and gather all the Vietnamese forces he had, and then meet the group at the same spot.

As the Team returned through the main gate, Corporal Hays briefed the Americal Division MP on duty of the situation so they could pass the word to have everyone on the lookout for Major Risner.

It seemed like forever before the group arrived at the office. While Captain Greenwold was making the appropriate calls, everyone geared up from the Group Guard with M-16s, fragmentary and smoke grenades and extra bandoliers of ammunition. This time, they had combat helmets, flak jackets, bayonets, etc., and Gunnery Sergeant Dick Petterson took charge.

The Team quickly drove back to the rendezvous point and found that the Popular Forces had already begun their search and rescue mission heading west towards the mountains. Armed to the teeth, the Team joined up with the other members of the Army Advisory Unit and began their own search of the area sweeping in a clockwise arc up to a kilometer away.

The villagers who had previously seen little or no military presence this close to their huts ignored the American forces. That really pissed Corporal Hays off. They knew something had happened but weren't talking. By dusk the Team had to quit and Staff Sergeant Cong was visibly weeping. By dark the next day, the PFs called off their search.

The next morning around 0600, Gunnery

Sergeant Petterson and Corporal Hays met and talked about all the possibilities of what could have happened to Major Risner but none of them had good endings. Neither Marine had slept through the night. Both Petterson and Hays went back and forth on Highway One in both directions a few times during that morning, but knew the chance of seeing him was remote. Everyone was hoping for a miracle.

Shortly after dark around 1800, Gunnery Sergeant Petterson showed up at the office. Everyone had left except for Hays and Cong. Motioning for Hays and Cong to follow him, Petterson made his way to the back of the hut. In a somber and quiet voice Petterson spoke to them. "You guys realize that someone has snatched the Major." Looking at Hays he said, "Gene you know the Major and I go way back." Hays nodded his head in agreement.

"I can't sit back and wait and hope that he will return. If they get him back up North and he is recognized they will execute him."

"Who would recognize...." Hays got out before Petterson raised his hand stopping him.

"The Major and I have done some things in the past that pissed off a whole bunch of folks. I can't go into details now but understand that if he is taken to Hanoi he will probably be killed."

"What can we do?" Hays and Cong said in unison.

"That's what I want to go over now and we must hurry."

It was 2145 hours when the Cerlist truck reached the main gate to An Tan. The Americal Division MP held his left hand out to halt the truck. Corporal Hays stopped even with the MP standing in front of a swinging gate arm.

"What's your business tonight Corporal?" the MP asked.

Hays recognized the MP as a Marine Private First Class who had been assigned from MAG-13 to augment the Americal Division Military Police. He had seen and talked to him several times over the last month.

"Private First Class Ramberg, how goes it?" Hays asked.

"Slow and boring. What are you doing out here at this time of night?" The MP had recognized Hays and relaxed his manner.

"Same ole shit. You remember our Interpreter, Staff Sergeant Cong, don't you?" Hays said referring to the Vietnamese Marine sitting in the shotgun seat.

"Yeah, I think so."

"We have some cement bags that Staff Sergeant Cong and I need to deliver to Ky Lien Elementary. We were supposed to do it earlier this afternoon so they can begin work on a new addition to the school but we forgot about it until now."

The MP aimed his spotlight in the back bed of the truck and saw the bags of cement.

"You know the gate closes at 2200 hours in 15 minutes. Can you get back here by then?"

"Maybe, but you're not going to keep us from

coming back if we are a little late are you?" Hays asked grinning while holding out $10 in MPC (Military Payment Certificates used as legal tender for the American dollar).

Private First Class Ramberg looked over his shoulder to see if the U.S. Army Sergeant behind him was paying any attention to what was going on and he wasn't; he took the bill in his hand.

"Okay, but make sure it's before 2400 when I am scheduled to be relieved."

"No sweat" Hays replied. "We'll be back within an hour."

The MP raised the arm on the gate and waved the truck through.

Mr. Pham was sipping on a glass of rice wine in front of his house when the truck pulled up. He recognized it immediately from the white stenciled writing on the side doors that read "MAG-12 Civic Action Team."

As Hays and Cong got out of the truck, Pham rose from his chair to greet them.

"I am delighted and surprised to see you both" Pham said smoothly with only a trace of an accent. "Is something wrong? Please come inside."

As he ushered them inside he did not detect the movement in the shadows of another figure that came behind them. He led them to a modest table that doubled as a desk and as a tea server. "Please sit. Have you heard anything more about Major Risner?" He asked with genuine concern.

"That's what we are here about," Hays replied.

Pham turned to Staff Sergeant Cong and spoke in Vietnamese. "I am afraid he may have been captured."

Cong: "I think so also but captured by whom, and where would he be?"

Pham shrugged his shoulders: "How could anyone know?"

Hays leaned forward in his chair. "Translate for me please. I think you said 'Khong Biet' or 'I don't know'?"

Pham nodded silently in assent.

A left hand suddenly reached around from behind Pham and grabbed him by the forehead. At the same time, a right hand brought a razor sharp K-Bar knife to Pham's throat.

"Wrong answer asshole!" said the voice behind him in a calm measured way that thoroughly frightened Pham.

"Petterson?" he asked recognizing the voice. "Why do you treat me......" he began to ask but Petterson didn't give him a chance to finish the sentence.

"Pham" he began, "You listen to me very carefully or you will be dead in a matter of seconds. Do you understand me?"

Pham began sweating profusely and was visibly shaken. He nodded his head in assent.

"Good because I'm not going to fuck around with you. I want to know where the Major is, now!" he said menacingly, still holding the knife blade to Pham's throat.

"Petterson, you know I would tell you if I knew. I am your friend," he pleaded.

"Second wrong answer Pham and he placed enough pressure on the knife blade to where a small trickle of blood began dripping down Pham's neck staining his linen white shirt.

"One more wrong answer and you are 30 seconds from Nirvana."

"Okay, okay. I know of a camp near the Laotian border. It was used by the Viet Minh during our war with the French. It's where we used to keep POWs. We called it Camp Dalat. However, I can't tell you for sure if he is being taken there. I can show you on the map," he said pointing to the regional map of Quang Ngai Province on the wall to his left.

"What else do you know Pham?" Petterson continued keeping the pressure on Pham's neck with the knife blade.

"Nothing else, I swear." Pham again pleaded.

"Bullshit Pham. You have contacts with everyone," Petterson countered. "Last chance." Slowly he moved the blade away from Pham's throat causing Pham to relax for a moment. Shaking his head from side to side to show he knew nothing else, Pham reached for a rag from the table in front of him. As his right hand reached the rag the K-Bar knife came straight down through the middle of his right hand pinning it to the table. Pham screamed in pain as blood spattered everywhere including on Hays and Cong. Staff Sergeant Cong looked in utter disbelief at Petterson, then at Hays and made a move to remove the knife blade from Pham's hand. Petterson deftly pushed Cong's hand away.

"Petterson, he knows nothing else!" Cong said passionately.

"The fuck he doesn't," he said, and Petterson removed his 45 pistol from his holster and put it against the temple of the now weeping Pham.

Cong: "Please Gunny Petterson, do not do this!"

Hays: "Tell him Pham, last chance!"

Cong: "Please, no! Don't kill him!"

Pham: "It's okay. Either way I will die."

Hays: "What do you mean either way, Pham?"

Pham: "I have a brother in Hanoi. We fought together as Viet Minh but he would not leave his family after the Communist take-over and come with me to South Vietnam. They threatened to kill him and his family and me if I didn't cooperate."

Hays: "Cooperate how? You mean you knew something was going to happen to Major Risner?"

Pham: "No, I swear I didn't know about his capture. I told them that you would be at Khoung Quang yesterday."

Petterson was still holding the pistol to Pham's head. "So he is alive, he was captured?"

Pham: "Yes, but I only found out about the plan the same day that it happened. I was instructed to make sure that someone was there that you knew and trusted."

Hays: "Phan Thi Lan! I saw her right after the Major went missing."

Pham: "Yes and she was threatened also. They told her they would kill her family if she didn't help."

Hays: "Who are they?"

Pham was groaning in pain. "NVA soldiers. They wore ARVN uniforms and drove an ARVN truck. That's what they took the Major in."

Hays: "Wait a minute. How did they know that Major Risner would come back to his vehicle to meet Major Nourse?'

Pham: "They didn't. I knew nothing about Major Nourse being there. You must have surprised them."

Hays: "How do you mean we surprised them?"

Pham: "They told me afterwards that the plan was to kill all the team members and take Major Risner captive."

Petterson: "But we showed up with too many people for that, right?" He lowered the pistol from Pham's head.

Pham: "Yes, that scared them from trying anything when you first arrived. They stayed around hoping that they might get another chance and they were very surprised to see the Major come back to his vehicle."

Hays: "So you were playing both sides making sure you were safe. You saw all this as it happened?"

Pham: "Yes, but from a distance. I was to warn them if any one from Ly Tin District Headquarters showed up."

Hays: "So you did know Major Nourse was supposed to be there also?"

Pham: "No, this is the first I heard about that."

Petterson: "Hold still, I'm going to take the knife out of your hand." Pham muffled a cry as the blade was removed. Petterson handed him the rag on the table to wrap around his hand.

"Show me on the map where this camp is."

"One more thing Petterson" Pham said.

"What's that?"

"The NVA officer told me that Major Risner was going to be taken to Hanoi and that they were looking forward to interrogating him."

Hays looking quizzically at Petterson: "Why would they be so interested in anything we're doing down here?"

Petterson looked at Hays with that "don't question me" look. "Probably just a bunch of talk, Pham. They probably think he's a pilot and they want to parade him in Hanoi."

Pham cradled his injured hand with his left. Bowing to Gunnery Sergeant Petterson he said, "I am so sorry Petterson to betray you."

"No time for that, Pham. Show me on the map where you think they will take him."

"It's a place close to Salavan across the Laotian border." Pham traced a path that he figured they would take. "They can only drive maybe 10 kilometers before they will have to continue on foot. It is rugged terrain and slow going. They have a day's head start on you if that's what you are thinking."

Petterson replied, "You don't know what I am thinking."

To Hays and Cong, Petterson said, "Let's saddle up and get the hell out of here."

Pham hung his head as the trio left through his door. They got into the Cerlist with Hays driving, Cong in the back and Petterson riding shotgun. Just as Hays turned the engine over, they heard the blast of a 45 pistol coming from Pham's house. No one said a word.

"Head south, Gene" Petterson said. "Keep an eye on the odometer and slow down when we get about 10 clicks down the road. I've got to find the Major or I am afraid they will kill him."

"Why is that?" Hays asked.

"Maybe some other day or time but not now."

Hays knew better than to press Petterson. The Gunny gave Hays instructions on what to do over the next 2 days. When they got to the point where Petterson wanted to stop, he told Hays to pull over on the side of the road.

Hays said, "Dick, I want to go with you."

Cong: "I do also. You need me to interpret for you."

Petterson: "I know both of you want to help but this has to be a one man mission. I've trained my whole life for this. Besides, I need you guys to cover for me."

"I will." Hays said.

Petterson reached in the back for his rucksack.

"Give me the flu, give me gonorrhea, give me anything you want but make sure they think I'm in my hooch in the bed sick."

Hays: "Will do."

Petterson began rubbing his face and head with

camouflage paint as well as all of his exposed extremities. He took off his jungle utility jacket and his cover. He strapped a cartridge belt around his waist with a canteen filled with water, a small flashlight with a red lens cover, first aid pouch, K-Bar knife, and a 45 caliber pistol with fully loaded magazine and two extra magazines of ammo.

"What about your M-16?" Hays asked.

"It will only slow me down," Petterson smiled. "You know the drill, right?"

"Yeah, I will return here at the rendezvous point every day at dusk for the next 2 days. If you're not back by the 3rd night I am to report you as MIA."

Petterson reached out and shook Hays' and Cong's hands.

"Semper Fi Marines" he said with a smile and then he disappeared into the night.

CAPTURED!

Major Risner walked back to the vehicles and after waiting a couple of minutes realized that Major Nourse must have forgotten about meeting him. Looking north Risner shielded his eyes from the hot midday sun and could see the Ly Tin District Headquarters a short distance away. Since no one was coming from that direction, his gaze focused on an ARVN truck about 200 meters up the road that was apparently having mechanical problems. Risner decided to drive his jeep to the District Headquarters to find Major Nourse, then he realized he didn't have the keys; Captain Greenwold had driven his jeep and had forgotten to give him the keys. So the Major started walking in the direction of Ly Tin District Headquarters.

He walked about half the distance to the ARVN truck past a couple of huts when a young Vietnamese girl who looked to be 7 to 9 years old ran up to him from the area of the truck. He was surprised to see that it was Phan Thi Lan, one of the girls he had sponsored for a scholarship. She seemed surprised to see him and spoke to him excitedly in English.

"Thieu ta," she began, "There is an accident on the railroad tracks," she said pointing in the direction of the ARVN truck. Without thinking, Major Risner ran the rest of the way up to the tracks and found a man laying face down in a ditch. He noticed several people gathered around with 4 ARVN soldiers standing over the man in the ditch. The soldiers beckoned him to help. As he began to kneel down to inspect the man's condition, the man suddenly rolled over on his back pointing a carbine directly up at Major Risner. He also felt a pistol placed at the back of his head. As he instinctively tried to move he was pistol whipped, disarmed and a gunnysack was thrown over his head. He was taken up the hill from the ditch he had been in and pushed onto his stomach in the back of a covered truck. They bound his wrists individually and then tied them together about 2 to 3 inches apart in front of him and tied the gunnysack around his neck. They conducted a thorough search of him and took all his personal possessions and papers including a notebook, his boot blousing bands, military driver's license, U.S. Armed Forced Identification Card, Geneva Convention Card, PX Ration Card and ID Tags (dog tags). The notebook contained information on a Civil Affairs meeting with Major Nourse that concerned Chu Lai's New Life Hamlet. Though dazed and in shock, Major Risner realized what was happening and was already trying to gather his senses, paying attention to where they were going if he got a chance to escape.

Though he couldn't see, there were 2 individuals in the back of the truck and 2 in the front. The ones in the rear placed their feet and rifles on the Major's back. The truck sped off and after two minutes or so crossed a bridge and then proceeded for another 3 minutes or so when the road became rough. About 5 minutes later, the truck turned right and proceeded down a steep incline. No one spoke. A moment later, one of the soldiers in the back raised the heel of his boot and stomped the Major in the small of his back producing a load groan which caused the other soldiers to laugh. Speaking normally now the soldiers engaged in humorous banter about how big the Major was and each would occasionally poke him with the barrels of their rifles. Any response from the Major brought more laughter.

The truck continued to move up and down steep inclines for another few minutes before stopping. Risner laid in the back of the truck for a couple of minutes before they let the tail gate down and they pushed his body out the back of the truck where he slumped to the ground. As he tried to sit up straight a rifle butt was thrust into his chest knocking him back to lying position. "You do as we say, you hear?" No response. This brought a kick to his side. "You hear, Marine?" No response. The captors laughed and talked some more. He could smell the smoke from cigarettes and instantly wished he had one. Then one of his captors raised him to an upright position, helped him stand and began to lead him down another steep incline placing a weapon across his chest to hold him up while walking downhill.

After walking for less than an hour, Major Risner was seated on the ground with his back against a wall. It was cool to his back and reeked of urine. He heard a lot of talking around him, recognizing the word Thieu Ta (Major) and knew they were talking about him. After a few minutes, someone came over to him and cut his jungle utility jacket off, leaving his white undershirt on. Then they led him inside a house and removed the gunnysack from his head for the first time. He was forced to his knees with his hands still bound in front of him. Adjusting his eyes, Risner saw he was in a room that contained a table with a single candle, behind which sat a slender male Vietnamese dressed in a NVA uniform.

He called the Major by name, mispronouncing it as "Reesner" (sic) and asked him what type of airplane he flew.

"My name is Richard F Risner, Serial Number 067619, Major, United States Marine Corps Reserve."

"What kind of airplane you fly?" The interrogator asked again. After receiving no answer, the interrogator hit the table hard with a round piece of bamboo about 2 feet long.

He then asked quickly, "How many helicopters are in Chu Lai? How many bombs did you drop?"

Risner realized that his captors had made the erroneous assumption that he was a pilot, probably because of the Forward Air Observer wings he wore above his left pocket before they cut his jacket off. What they didn't know was that during his tour of duty in Vietnam, he had flown a total of 41 missions in different aircraft including assignments as a Bombardier/Navigator in A-6's, a Radar Intercept Officer in F4's, and as a Spotter in both TA-4F's and 01 and 02 Spotter Aircraft. Risner had also participated in 5 Rolling Thunders over Hanoi and Hai Phong Harbor before Operation Arc-Lite. He knew it was better for his captors to think of him as a pilot because they would dare not kill him to collect their bounty. The bounty was somewhere around $300-$500 American. That was 5 to 10 times the average yearly wage for a farmer. The bad news was that they would surely try to transport him to the Hanoi Hilton where they proudly displayed their captured trophies to the rest of the North Vietnamese Army and people.

After again refusing to answer the last questions, the interrogator moved around the table and hit him in the side with the bamboo stick. The interrogator then looked at him and said, "You are from Chicago, Illinois".

He stated this as a fact and not as a question. This startled Major Risner that they somehow knew his place of birth. Then he remembered his captors had taken his wallet and realized this information was on his government driver's license. The interrogator then asked him:

"What kinds of helicopters are in Chu Lai?"

Receiving no response again, the interrogator switched the bamboo rod to his left hand and with his right pulled a knife from his belt. Risner expected to be cut. Smiling, the NVA soldier pointed the knife at his throat then hooked the end of the knife under Risner's t-shirt, ripping the shirt down the front.

"Oh, look here" he said switching the rod back into his right hand and the knife in his left. He poked Risner with the bamboo rod in a place where his appendix scar was visible. The appendix scar amused the interrogator and he delighted in poking him there.

He then asked Major Risner 3 times in quick

succession, "What type of airplane do you fly?"

This time when Risner didn't answer, the interrogator hit him twice in the groin area with the bamboo rod, doubling Risner over in pain. He lost sight of the interrogator and heard what seemed to him to be some type of argument taking place. Then a second interrogator appeared. He was a very short Vietnamese Elder who introduced himself as Mr. Tahung. He was fluent in English, polite in manner and spoke as though well educated. He was well dressed in casual attire and exuded a hint of some sweet smelling cologne. He stood in front of Risner.

"I am sorry to inconvenience you." He smiled. He then pulled another chair from the side of the desk and helped Risner get to his feet and then into the chair.

"I apologize for the actions of my compatriot." He stopped for a moment and reached into a shirt pocket for a cigarette. Risner noted that it was a French brand popular with the Vietnamese. After lighting it, he took a big drag and exhaled.

"I would like to speak to you as one professional to another." Not waiting for a response he continued.

"It is indeed unfortunate that your President, a capitalistic warmonger, would order you to fight a revolution that is not your war." He paused for a moment and offered the end of his cigarette to Risner who shook his head no.

"The peoples of the world want peace and your people want peace also." He paused again for effect.

"Isn't it an awful thing that we have to be

fighting one another in a people's revolution that is not in your part of the world?" Not getting a response he continued.

"I know Mr. Agnew was the Republican candidate for Vice-President." He took another drag off the cigarette and snuffed it out in an ash tray on the desk behind him.

"I am certain your Commanding Officer does not agree with this war that involves the people's revolution." He moved slightly backwards and sat with one of his butt cheeks on the corner of the desk.

"Are you aware of the student uprisings in Kentucky, Ohio and California?"

Risner again said nothing.

"Wouldn't you and your compatriots like to meet to discuss peace in a more pleasant atmosphere?" He smiled.

"You must be aware that the United States was forewarned by the French and other allied forces that they should not involve so many people so far away from home?"

Risner was surprised that his interrogator was so knowledgeable of current affairs in the States. Mr. Tahung then offered him a cup of a hot and bitter tea. He held the cup up to the Major's mouth allowing him to drink. At first Risner was afraid that they might try to drug or poison him but he knew he was becoming badly dehydrated and needed the liquid. He drank the tea to the bottom of the cup.

"You see," Tahung began, "We can be friends if we cooperate with each other."

Tahung returned to the desk where he once again sat on the corner. He took out another cigarette and lit it this time not offering Risner a drag. After inhaling and exhaling a puff, he looked into Risner's eyes intently.

"You can have this pack if you cooperate with me," he said smiling. Risner said nothing.

"Have you ever been to Korea, Major Risner?" he said disarmingly. As Risner stiffened, a cold chill went up his spine and he could not mask the surprise on his face.

"My name is Richard F. Risner, Serial Number 067619, Major, United States Marine Corps Reserve."

"So, you think we do not know these things?" Tahung asked rhetorically.

Tahung waited for a response smoking his cigarette as he waited. After a couple of minutes he continued, trying to goad the Major.

"You have nothing to say about your War crimes?" Tahung asked.

"My name is Richard F. Risner...." He got out before Tahung held his hand up in a dismissing fashion.

"Save it for another time, Major" he said smiling. Then changing his tone and expression in a menacing manner, he said: "You will find out later that the Geneva Convention will not save you."

Mr. Tahung turned and then went to the back of the room where another heated argument ensued between him and the first interrogator. It was obvious from the discussion that Mr. Tahung was in charge. After a few minutes, the arguing stopped, two soldiers appeared and Major Risner was lifted from the chair by both arms by two of his original captors. He was taken outside and placed in a kneeling position where they dislocated both arms from his shoulders to keep him from using them. He tried not to cry out in pain as they took a large wooden pole and inserted it under his armpits and tied his useless arms to the pole. They took his jungle boots off and removed his socks. They beat his feet with bamboo sticks laughing about how big they were (he wore a size 12). After a few minutes they gave his boots back to him minus the shoestrings because none of them could wear them. After they put his boots back on him, one of his captors smashed all his toes on both feet with a metal hammer to discourage him from running. In excruciating pain Risner went back and forth in and out of consciousness. They had already cut off his shirt and undershirt. His belt was removed and not returned. During this humiliation, his captors jabbed him in the groin several times and beat him about the chest and back and his legs with bamboo sticks. While in a forward hunched position, local villagers were brought to him and were encouraged by his captors to urinate and defecate on him.

One of the women brought a baby boy close to his face and allowed the baby to urinate in his face. After a long period of abuse and torture, his captors replaced the sack over his head, tied it around his neck and popped his arms back into his shoulder sockets, causing him to walk with his chest protruding.

With a tether tied around his neck, he was then

led off by 5 Viet Cong guerillas down a gradual incline that eventually leveled out. One of the VC pulled the Major along by the tether. This VC was dressed in a black, long sleeved shirt, a straw "coolie" type hat and black shorts. Most of the other VC were similarly attired except for some with cloths tied around their heads instead of a hat. Though blinded by the hood, Major Risner surmised that the man in charge was the one leading him because he was giving all the orders.

They marched during the rest of the night over rough terrain. Major Risner had sensed that at times they were going through narrow passages in single file formation. He had been warned to keep quiet and his captors seldom said anything. If he tripped or fell or was not moving fast enough they would beat him about the legs or poke him in the groin. His upper torso was bare and the undergrowth scratched him. They would wade across small streams filling his boots with water chafing his feet as he struggled to keep walking. He could feel and hear his broken toes squishing in his boots. Upon entering a camp area, the VC who was leading Major Risner called another VC over and told him in English that his prisoner was a Major and a pilot.

"See what I have brought you," he said as pulled the sack off Risner's head.

"This is Honcho," he said to Risner referring to the other VC leader. Honcho looked at Major Risner and spit in his face and then reached back to hit him. The VC leading Risner stopped Honcho before he could hit Major Risner and then moved Risner through the camp and set him down under a tree. Honcho returned later, replaced the sack over the Major's head and using the wooden pole under the Major's armpits, he proceeded to dislocate both shoulders again, leaving him hunched over from the waist up.

Honcho placed his face in front of Risner's and through the hood told him: "You will need your strength for the trip ahead. Sleep well Major." And with that Honcho hit Risner up the side of his head with his pistol. Risner fell unconscious. Emotionally and physically drained he fell into a deep sleep.

When Risner awoke he could tell by the lack of light through his hood that it must have been near dusk. He could hear the others in the camp talking about him, hearing the word Thieu ta. Pretending sleep he tried to absorb as much as he could about what he could hear and smell. He heard a radio come to life but couldn't understand what they were saying.

Honcho: (in Vietnamese) "Yes, we have him. We will leave in about an hour."

On the other end: "The helicopter will be waiting for you at the rendezvous point. Make sure he stays alive. Our Chinese Comrades are looking forward to meeting with him. No mistakes, do you understand?"

Honcho: "Yes, Sir. We will have him there at the appointed time."

Comrade Colonel Wong tu Chen of the Red Chinese Army was standing next to the NVA Commander General Giap when he put down the phone.

Giap: "It is all arranged. The helicopter will pick him up from our rendezvous camp in Laos within the next 8 hours."

With a slight formal bow Chen said: "Comrade General, I thank you for your assistance in this matter. We could not believe our luck when we saw his picture in the <u>Stars and Stripes</u> newspaper. It is fortunate that the Americans are stupid enough to put their officers' pictures in their newspapers."

General Giap: "I agree. I must admit though I was surprised to find you are interested in such a low level officer and that someone was able to identify him."

Chen: "That someone is me and I vividly remember that face and the hand pointing a pistol at my head. His comrade also called him by his name, Risner. Of course he was not a good shot and for that I am thankful."

Giap: "And if I may ask, how did that happen?"

Chen: "Let me tell you what happened in Korea in the summer of 1955.

THE SEARCH

Petterson moved swiftly and silently as he headed into the undergrowth of the jungle. He tried to stay on a path but it was difficult to navigate in the dark undergrowth. He periodically checked his compass and watch, both on a wristband and both glowed in the dark. He was heading in a West-South-West direction on a straight line towards the camp Pham had shown him on his map. Not thinking about what he might encounter he drove himself with the thought of freeing Major Risner and concern over what they were doing to him.

After covering over a kilometer by his reckoning, he began to climb by small degrees. Coming to a clearing on the side of a small hill, he instantly saw what looked like a procession of lights winding around the hill. They were moving towards his direction. Petterson instantly knew that they were VC or more likely NVA troops using candles to light their way as they made their movements during the night. Their tactics consisted of using the night and stealth to cover and stage themselves as they prepared for battle on an unsuspecting enemy.

As the lights came closer Petterson retreated back into the undergrowth and observed the column of what looked like to be about 2 dozen soldiers on the march. They were moving in a north easterly direction away from Petterson. He decided to wait about 15 minutes to give them time to move on without detecting him. Moving forward to the same trail that the soldiers had left, Petterson began to move faster. With the memory of Pham's map etched in his brain he knew he was heading the right way towards the camp. Staying to the sides of the trail and weaving back and forth he was on the constant lookout for trouble. It came about half a kilometer from where he started. He almost stepped into the punji pit but he realized it when the ground under his boot began to give way, giving him a split-second warning to jump or go around. He continued moving and kept his vision focused to the sides of the trail, constantly scanning the ground in front of him all at the same time. He felt it before he saw it or smelled it or heard it. Instinctively he went to the prone position on the ground straining to hear what he felt. He heard the distinct muted sounds of voices talking in the distance; he figured no more than 50 meters away. Raising his head he could see the reflection of a small fire against a large boulder and a thin column of smoke rising from it. He thought that he heard at least 2 voices and he fixed their position at 30 degrees to his right. Rising slightly to his knees and then to a crouching position, he moved to the left off the trail and into the undergrowth. He barely had enough room to maneuver as he was in the middle of a thicket and the thickets lined the path on both sides. Surveying his surroundings Petterson figured there was no way to go around this outpost without being seen or heard. He thought that he heard the sound of a small stream or brook ahead and he hoped that by staying close to the stream it would muffle any noise he might make. Moving slowly, keeping his bearings, he reached the stream and cupped his hands to take his first drink of water since beginning his trek. He decided to discard the canteen as the sloshing water and bulk of it might give his presence away. Hearing the voices more distinctly and seeing the illumination of the small fire, he thought he saw the shadows of two slightly built men. There was no doubt they were the enemy as no U.S. or ARVN troops were even close to being located near this spot. There were no villages or rice paddies as this was a remote jungle area leading to higher mountains to the border with Laos.

Petterson knew if Risner and his captors made it through the mountains in Laos that Major Risner wouldn't be able to escape his fate in Hanoi or China. He couldn't allow that to happen. Looking upstream the water seemed to follow the path to the side of the campfire. It would make sense that the outpost would be located near a source of water and close enough to observe any unwanted guests and at the same time provide a place to rest and recuperate their own forces. Petterson tested the water which rose only ankle high to his boots. He started moving forward slowly listening ahead as well as monitoring any noise he might be making. The stream seemed to muffle his movements so he continued moving through the stream in a crouched position. He slowly drew his K-Bar knife from its sheath gripping it in his left hand. At the same time, he slowly and quietly undid the snap on his holster flap and held his .45 pistol at the ready. He kept moving at a slow pace watching all around him when his left boot gave way to a sink hole. Before it could trap his foot he deftly raised it as high as he could and planted it back where his right foot was. Never taking his eyes off the objective he probed with his K-Bar knife into the water ahead. The sink hole was between two rocks no bigger than soccer balls but the stream bed on either side seemed solid. Straddling the rocks he looked like a rodeo rider with his legs in a wishbone. He came within ten meters of the two figures and dropped even lower. Judging by their black pajamas and coolie hats he took them to be VC. While they were not battle hardened NVA troops they could be just as lethal. They sat across from each other with the fire in the middle. The one directly in front of Petterson had his back to him shielding the VC opposite him. Petterson knew what he had to do instinctively. Swapping his K-Bar and pistol between left and right hands, he paused for a few moments letting his eyes get adjusted and he listened to make sure there was no one else. The two voices continued with laughing back and forth. Satisfied there were only these two, Petterson edged forward to within a couple of meters of the first VC, hidden from view from the other VC by the back of the one directly in front of him.

Pausing momentarily, Petterson moved up quickly behind the first, reached around to the front with his K-Bar and slashed the man's throat from left to right. In the same fluid motion he brought the knife handle back to his ear and flung it at the other VC piercing him in the heart before he could do or say anything. He died with the look of surprise in his eyes. Petterson switched his pistol back into his right hand as he surveyed the area with his 45 pointed straight in front of him. He remained behind the first VC who had slumped forward after his throat was cut, listening for any other sounds. There were none. Petterson holstered his pistol and went to the other VC and removed his K-Bar from the VC's chest. He cleaned it on the shirt of his victim. Looking into the small fire Petterson could see a small pot resting on a stone near the edge of the fire. Feeling some hunger pangs suddenly, he reached for the thin wire handle of the pot. "Shit!" he cursed silently as his fingers slightly touched the hot handle. Sticking them back into the stream to cool then off he drew his K-Bar again and brought the pot back to the stream where he cooled it off. Removing the lid there contained about 2 cups of white rice. Muttering to himself "Why the fuck not?" he reached in with his fingers and shoveled the rice into his mouth and finished it in less than 5 minutes. His hunger and thirst satiated for the time being, Petterson urinated into the campfire and spoke to the two corpses lying in front of him.

"Hate to eat and run guys but I've got places to go to people to see, you know how it is!" With that, he quickly continued down the trail.

JOURNEY TO DALAT

As the light of day turned to the dark of night, Major Risner was led away by a new group of three Viet Cong except for the one leading him, Honcho. Because of Risner's height and incapacity with his arms in and out of their sockets and his toes smashed, Honcho decided it would be easier for him to lead Risner if he tied the tether to his hands rather than around his neck. Honcho popped Risner's arms back into his shoulder sockets and had his guards remove the pole from underneath his armpits. Then they retied Risner's hands in front with a heavy corded rope and placed the hood back over his head. Risner had looked at Honcho defiantly before having the hood placed over his head so Honcho rewarded him with a swift blow to his gut with a bamboo rod. Honcho took over leading Risner. They had not traveled very far when it started to rain. Ever mindful of his need to escape Risner knew he had to make an escape attempt even if it cost him his life, so he waited for the right opportunity. The constant prodding and whipping continued until he hardly felt it any more. His trousers were tattered from the constant rubbing against barbs of thickets as well as the beating he was taking from the guards. They went up a hill for a short distance, and then descended down another incline for an undetermined distance until they reached level ground. As they crossed one stream that was knee deep, it started raining more heavily. The terrain to their right was high and steep. The rain intensified and made the trail along the stream slippery. As they crossed another stream, Honcho slipped and let go of the rope tether. Major Risner fell into the stream along with Honcho. He managed to lift the sack tied around his neck sufficiently to see what little he could of his surroundings. Honcho was nowhere to be seen. Risner then stayed underwater moving downstream and he crossed to the far bank. He then backed into the stream bank and hid under some shrubs. He could hear the VC talking excitedly as they tried to find him. It was still raining heavily and visibility in the dark was nil. As one VC was prodding the brush with his rifle, near where the Major was hiding, Risner reached up grabbing the VC's rifle barrel with his large hands pulling him down where he managed to grab him around the neck still with wrists bound. He dragged his captor into the stream and held his head under water. Major Risner continued to hold the VC under water until he was sure he was dead. The sounds of the rain and the running stream muffled any sound made by the two antagonists. As Risner lifted the head above water, he saw it was Honcho.

Risner pushed the body in front of him farther downstream until it got shallower and then crossed over to the other side where the water was deeper. He then went back upstream to find the trail where they originally entered, as he figured they would be looking for him downstream.

Major Risner lay· in the stream for a long time until he was sure that the VC had stopped looking for him. When he finally crawled out of the stream he tried to locate the trail but was unable to do so. He reentered the stream and continued upstream until the water got shallow and then he crawled out. He hid in the brush and tried to rest until daylight. He did not want to fall asleep and get caught again so he started rubbing his bindings on his wrists against the rough bark of a tree near him. It was a slow painful process as the rubbing not only wore against his bindings but also chafed his hands and lower arms.

Trying a different tactic, he carefully looked around then crawled in the prone position towards the stream looking for a sharp rock. Just as he reached the stream he heard the click. One of the VC guards must have heard him rubbing his bindings against the tree and the guard had moved behind him by just a meter.

The Russian SKS he was holding misfired. A round was stuck between the chamber and the stripper clip and it jammed the rifle. As the VC guard stared stupidly at his weapon he gave Risner the time he needed to extend his legs and kick the guard's feet out from under him and he landed heavily face first. Momentarily dazed, Risner placed the VC's head in a vise grip between his two boots and he twisted until he heard the neck snap.

"Two down, two to go" he said silently to himself. Reaching the guard's body he located the folding bayonet on the SKS and cut the rope binding his wrists. His hands were numb from the loss of blood as he rubbed them together trying to get the feeling back. He searched the guard's body and found 4 more stripper clips of ammo and 2 hand grenades. Searching the guard's shirt he found a pocket on the inside in which there was a small pack of Pall Malls and a short book of matches wrapped in plastic that were the same kind as those contained in the C-Rations American troops were issued.

"Probably taken from an American POW or KIA," Risner thought to himself. "I have a hard time getting these at the PX. Thanks Charley, you SOB." He then dragged the guard's body into the stream and watched it float away. The rain was still coming down hard as he moved back into the undergrowth and listened again for the other 2 guards. He thought to himself that the other 2 had probably gone downstream and by now had seen at least one of the bodies. Once they saw that they would correctly surmise he was upstream. Thinking he had a few minutes before they would reach his position he decided to let them do the work and find him, rather than Risner trying to find them. He now had an equalizer with the rifle and grenades. Suddenly remembering the rifle had jammed, he slid the bolt back and removed the jammed round. Not taking any chances he removed the stripper clip in case it was damaged and reloaded the weapon with one of the clips taken off the guard's body. Letting the bolt slide home Risner was confident the rifle would fire when needed.

Fortunately the Team had acquired 6 of the same type weapon from a local CAP unit who had a collection of enemy weapons captured from dead enemy soldiers or discovered in hidden caches. Each of the Team members had fired the weapons as well as

Chi-Com (Chinese Communist) and Russian AK-47s. Acquired meant that in exchange for the captured weapons the Team had given up 4 captured NVA flags. The flags had a red background with gold star in the middle and were about 3'X4'. All had bullet holes through them along with red blood stains and they reeked of body odors as well as urine. They were all captured flags-captured by Gunnery Sergeant Dick Petterson who had sewn each one using material from the H&MS-12 Para Loft (Parachute Rigging Loft) and an electric Japanese sewing machine.

Risner suddenly thought of Petterson. "Are you out there Dick?" he thought to himself. He knew if the situation were reversed he would be looking for Petterson. Satisfied that the guards weren't imminent he pulled out the Pall Malls and lit one taking a deep drag. He almost laughed out loud when he read the label: "Cigarettes may be hazardous to your health." He cupped his hands to hide the lighted match and the smoke and to protect it from the rain. There wasn't any smoke exhaled as he deeply inhaled each drag. His nicotine levels replenished, he finished half of the cigarette, snubbed the end out against his boot and returned the half a cigarette to its package and placed it inside one of the trouser pockets he had left. He had no sooner done this when he heard the remaining guards approaching. The rain had slackened a bit and his ears were fine tuned to the sounds of the underbrush. He was convinced that the last 2 guards were together. From a sitting position, ankles crossed, Risner raised the rifle to his shoulder resting his left hand under the barrel receiver group and his left elbow to his knee to steady the weapon; the classic sitting and firing position. The last 2 VC were slowly walking in single file about 3 meters apart. They were moving cautiously seemingly in slow motion listening for any sounds that their former captive might make. Risner waited patiently until he had the best shot he could take. Centering his sights on the 1st VC in line he waited until he was 10 meters away and Risner aimed at the upper chest of his former captor. He squeezed off the round dropping the soldier instantly. Risner cursed when the gun jammed as he tried to squeeze off a second round to take out the second guard. The VC looked in his direction briefly and ran off the opposite way. Risner quickly cleared the weapon hoping he wouldn't have to use it again. When he was convinced that the other guard had decided to leave, Risner went over to the VC he had killed. Searching the VC's body he found what looked like a marijuana cigarette which he discarded. Tucked in the waist band of his black trousers was a small snub nose 38 caliber revolver identical to the type that American pilots were issued. It was jokingly called a 50 shot revolver as it was normally good for about 50 shots before becoming completely unreliable. The gun had five rounds in it, and he couldn't find any more ammo on the VC's body.

"Time to go home" Risner said softly. Trying to focus on what he had to do next, he was tired and hungry but knew he had to make the most out of whatever darkness was left. He could hide out and sleep during the day.

NLF HEADQUARTERS HANOI

"What do you mean he escaped?" Giap said loudly into his phone. "What about the guards, where are they?" He listened for a minute shaking his head. "Execute that last guard and whoever they report to." He paused momentarily. "I don't care if Captain Xuan is the nephew of the Minister of the Interior. Do as I ordered, now!" and he hung up the phone. Comrade Colonel Chen could only shake his head as General Giap threw up his arms in complete disgust.

"What can I do?" General Giap said to Chen. "Who is this American Marine that I must sacrifice 4 of my soldiers and a nephew of the Minister of the Interior?"

Chen answered: "I told you what happened when I was the Camp Commander of Diaoyu Island and that Risner killed another American. What I didn't tell you was the American was a nuclear physicist. He was considered an expert on nuclear fission and the atomic bomb. We were going to team him up with our top rocket scientist Tsien Hsue-Shen." Chen went on to explain the importance of pairing up the American defector known simply as John with Tsien.

"Tsien was driven out of the United States in 1955. He was born in China and educated at MIT (Massachusetts Technical Institute) in 1935 and was a brilliant student. He was instrumental in the founding of the jet propulsion laboratory in California. He worked closely with the Aerojet corporation in the development of the first JATO (jet assisted take-off) and sounding rockets built in the United States. He interviewed Wernher von Braun and other members of the German V-2 rocket team in Germany. When Tsien returned to the United States from Germany in 1937, he edited the 800 page Jet Propulsion Manual that became the bible for post-war aircraft and rocket technical research in the post-war United States. By 1949, he designed a practical intercontinental rocket transport that could carry ten passengers from California to New York in 45 minutes!"

He further explained that by 1950, Tsien was undergoing a personal struggle of loyalty and allegiances between the motherland and the United States. On the one hand, Tsien married the cosmopolitan daughter of a senior military adviser to Chiang Kai-shek in 1947, applied to become a US citizen in 1949, and had become one of the senior scientists advising the US military on post-war development of rocket technology. He had begun pioneering highly secret work on the use of nuclear rocket engines. On the other hand, Tsien was revolted by the corruption of the Chinese nationalists, faced racial discrimination in the United States, and constantly vacillated in his desire to return to his homeland. He, like other Chinese scientists in the United States, began to receive letters from their relatives indicating hardships awaited them unless their expatriate son returned to the motherland.

Because of all the suspicion and paranoia about the Chinese Communists, Tsien lost his security clearance and was held under virtual house arrest from the middle of 1950 until 1955. He was returned to China as part of a deal for return of American prisoners held by the Chinese from World War II and the Korean War. American experts believed at the time that Tsien had been sufficiently absent long enough from the scientific community to make him ineffectual if he was returned to China.

Chen continued: "While Tsien was being held, the American defector known as John was being educated and trained under the direct supervision of Robert Oppenheimer. He participated in the development and improvement of the next generation of atomic bombs from the first bombs dropped over Japan to end World War II."

"So how did you capture him?" Giap asked.

"We didn't. He came over to our side willingly. It seemed his parents who were also scientists had secretly joined the American Communist Party. They believed in Socialism and that the greater good of man was served by the State. Their son followed suit and after seeing the results of the destruction of Hiroshima and Nagasaki decided he would learn as much as he could and then sell himself to the highest bidder. By this time the Soviets had already developed the technology and we were the highest bidders. Additionally the man's parents were eventually arrested for their involvement with the American Communist Party and accused of selling secrets to the Soviets. We capitalized on the situation and convinced him his government no longer cared about him or his family.

He was easily seduced."

"So the loss of the American delayed your development of a nuclear weapon?" Giap asked.

"Yes, by almost 10 years. However, our leadership never intended to use it as anything but a deterrent. Until we detonated our first atomic bomb in 1964, we risked the chance of being attacked by the Soviet Union or the United States without fear of reprisal," Chen answered. "We are now co-equals with all the other nations with nuclear capabilities."

"So should I put a pistol in my mouth now that we failed in capturing the Marine Major?" Giap said smilingly.

"No, my superiors will understand that your men were not successful in capturing him alive and that he died trying to escape. Hopefully his picture will not appear again in the American newspapers."

Giap smiled wanly.

CAMP DALAT

At Camp Dalat, sadistically named for the resort city in South Vietnam, 13 American prisoners of war languished in 4 foot by 6 foot bamboo cages. They were emaciated and the stench in and around them was unbearable even to their captors. Every morning at dawn, hands and feet hobbled by rope, they were forced to stand beside one another in formation while the NVA flag was raised and the bugler played their version of reveille. The prisoners were ordered to salute which they never did even though they were often beaten. Once the brief ceremony was over they were returned to their cages.

Once a week if their captors were in a good mood, they would give them a bucket of water from the well to wash themselves, with any water remaining to be used to clean their cages, normally covered with vomit or excrement. Lately the guards had not been in a good mood and it had been 3 weeks since they had been given any water to clean themselves.

This particular morning, the rain had stopped and the sun was shining. As the guards released the prisoners from their cages they seemed to be extremely agitated. The senior POW, Commander Rocky Bertilson, United States Navy, was from Newport News, Virginia. He had been shot down in his F-8U Crusader after veering over the Laotian border. A MIG-17 operating out of Phnom Penh made the mistake of engaging Bertilson's aircraft while ground troops were engaged in a battle with a hard core NVA battalion around Quang Ngai. While the MIG-17 was easily dispatched by Bertilson he could not escape the SAM missile that tore off the top of his tail and forced him to eject.

Commander Bertilson and the other 12 POWs all knew what the source of agitation was with the camp guards. Earlier the night before one of the guards who normally transported newly captured POWs to the camp returned alone. There had been a lot of shouting and all the camp guards gathered around him. Unbeknownst to the guards, the only enlisted POW in the camp knew how to speak and understand Vietnamese fluently. Sergeant Randall Owens, United States Marine Corps from Lafayette Mississippi, was an interrogator translator. He had been through a 52 week course in Vietnamese Language Training at the Defense Language Institute at the Presidio of Monterey in Monterey California. He was assigned to the 1st CAG and had been captured after his CAP unit had been overrun. His squad of 12 Marines had all been killed by an NVA force of over 100 men who had been tipped off by one of the village chiefs as to the Marines presence. Sergeant Owens was shot in the right arm and left leg and he still limped from the bullet that remained in his leg. Wisely, Sergeant Owens kept his language abilities hidden from his captors and he interpreted everything he heard and passed it on to Commander Bertilson in a made up code devised by the senior POW. In turn, each POW passed it on to another. What Sergeant Owens heard from the sole surviving guard was that a Marine Major by the name of Risner had escaped from his captors and had killed all the other guards including Honcho. After the guard told of his escape from Major Risner, the Camp Commander Major Than Le Phuoc immediately went to his radio shack where the message was sent to Hanoi. After less than 5 minutes, Major Phuoc went directly to the returning guard, pulled his pistol from his holster and promptly shot the guard through the forehead. Turning his attention to his executive officer, Captain Xuan, he summarily executed him with a shot to his left temple. Even the camp guards had been surprised and shocked when Xuan was shot. So all the POWs knew what happened from Sergeant Owens through their grapevine.

As they lined up for the morning formation they somberly waited until the bugler finished reveille. Commander Bertilson gave the command, "Attention!" followed by the order "Present Arms!" Each of the POWs rendered a hand salute. Major Phuoc was actually smiling. Then each of the prisoners began to sing "God Bless America." The Camp Commander was infuriated. Phuoc immediately went to Commander Bertilson, spit in his face and pistol whipped him to unconsciousness. Upon his command each of the guards began to beat the rest of the POWs using rifle butts. Later, in terrific pain and suffering from the beating he received, Commander Bertilson thought to himself that it was all worth it. All the other POWs felt the same way because Honcho, the VC leader Major Risner had killed, was the worst tormentor of the American POWs at Camp Dalat and they were deliriously happy that he had been killed. The name of Risner became a call to duty and honor and hope.

POINT OF NO RETURN

Gunnery Sergeant Petterson made another 5 kilometers before daybreak. He carefully secluded himself in a tall field of elephant grass and bamboo under a large tree next to a stream and went to sleep. It was a practiced, guarded sleep as he would waken instantly to any sound or movement out of the ordinary. The movement came at the bottom of his feet. Without moving a muscle, he opened his eyes and craned his neck forward and found himself staring into the eyes and mouth of a Malayan Pit Viper. If Petterson moved or the Viper moved any closer, he would surely be bitten.

Planning his movement carefully he readied his right boot to kick the Viper away and he hoped the Viper would retreat. In a quick motion that the Viper reacted to, Petterson kicked the Viper with his right boot just below its head but not before the Viper sank its fangs into the ankle webbing portion of his jungle boot. The snake was hurled back and slithered away. At first Petterson thought he had only felt the pressure of the snake's fangs. Untying his boot and pulling his sock down to his heel he discovered the two small puncture wounds. He didn't know how much venom he received but the area around his ankle had already turned red and he felt a partial paralysis around his ankle. He pulled his sock up and put his boot back on before the swelling would make that impossible. He unlaced his boots and looped the boot strings through the top two eyelets below the lacing grommets and tied them just above the top of his boots. Next he found a stick about ½" in diameter and he cut one of the ends off to about 6" in length with his K-Bar. He placed the stick inside the laces and began to twist the stick as hard as he could to cut off circulation to his foot. He sat there for a moment longer keeping an eye in the direction of where the snake had crawled off. He thought about his options.

"I won't be any good to Rich if I'm dead. I can't stay here because no one except some VC or NVA troops will find me. If I try to go either way I could die from the snake poisoning. My gut tells me to go back to where the trail left off leading to where I began. I'm sorry Rich, I tried."

His mind began to reel from the effects of the venom. He was back in Korea with Risner. They were talking in the submarine after completing their mission. Alone in the sub Captain's quarters changing clothes, Petterson asked Risner, "How well did you know that guy?"

"I knew him for the three years we spent in high school together. We weren't close friends. I was playing football, while he was active in the Honor Society and MENSA. He was a loner for the most part and considered a geek by many. After graduation we went our separate ways and I did not see him again before today."

"Well they obviously knew he wouldn't come with us willingly. I knew something was wrong when we saw he wasn't being guarded. Granted, he probably didn't have the means to escape and nowhere to go but when he pulled that pistol out there was no doubt in my mind that he defected."

Risner nodded his head in agreement. "By not telling me the truth they ensured that one of us would kill him."

Petterson asked "If you had known the truth would you have still shot him?"

As Risner began to answer, Petterson's mind shifted suddenly to the shooting and the sudden appearance of the Red Chinese officer afterwards. The Chinese officer's face was filled with hate and anger. He was chasing both Marines to the raft. Petterson kept looking behind him, he was gaining on them. Redfeather was pumping rounds into his chest but still he came. Just as they reached the raft, Risner turned and the Chinese officer raised his pistol to kill him. Petterson was yelling "No, no!" His head swirling and delirious, Petterson willed himself to get up and move. He began to head back to where he started. He took just a few steps when he stopped. Turning around, and ready to pass out, at the top of his voice he said, "Ain't no fucking way I'm abandoning you Rich, and if any of you black pajama mother fuckers want to stop me, come and get it!" And he turned back in the direction towards the camp.

THE REUNION

Finding a place by a stream and a trail that ran parallel to it, Major Risner took small mouthfuls of the stream water by hand to quench his thirst. He knew it could be contaminated but he needed the hydration. Though still cold from the water, it helped numb his wounds, so he returned to the water. He found some plants that looked edible and ate their bitter roots. He knew he needed strength if he was going to survive. All the training he received was helping him now. He ate insects and would have eaten raw fish if he could have caught one. He ate until his stomach told him no more. Then he was bloated and before much longer began to cramp. Not wanting to soil his trousers he removed them. They were torn in several places due to his ordeal and he used the opportunity to tear the legs off below the knee. It would help him during his running.

He took the rope that bonded his wrists together and unraveled it to use as thread. For a needle he found a sharp edged rock that he used to cut holes in his trousers. He could see the red marks all over his legs from where they beat him, but he didn't feel them now. Then the diarrhea began. As his bowels loosed, he found himself trying to hide the bubbles that gurgled up to the surface. Inwardly he laughed about it. He continued to move upstream. Nightfall approaching, he left the stream to get closer to the trail. When he was 5 meters from the trail in the underbrush, he saw about 20

Vietnamese moving on the trail carrying pots and baskets on bamboo poles and on their heads. As they approached his location, Major Risner hid farther back in the underbrush. At one point one of the Vietnamese women was only an arm's length away from him. They came to the stream, drank some water and then after resting a short time, returned to the trail and left. Major Risner stayed in that position until it got dark and then moved out to the trail once more. He was unable to orient himself, so he went back to the underbrush and tried to sleep through the night.

When he woke again at daybreak, Risner wandered around trying to find the trail or stream but he wandered off course and became disoriented due to his physical deterioration. As he continued through the thicket it began to thin out and then he saw a boy herding some water buffalo and followed him a distance until he came upon another stream. He stopped to drink some of the stream water, and he also ate some green berries that caused him to vomit. He followed the stream for a long distance until he saw another trail and some open fields. He thought he could hear aircraft flying in the distance and then saw one helicopter fly overhead. He ran into the open field but the aircraft never saw him. He thought that he saw some people running towards him about 300 meters away so he went back into the stream and hid once more.

After he was sure the people were gone, Major Risner continued following the stream hoping it would lead him back to the main road where they had left the

ARVN truck. From the aircraft he heard overhead, he knew he must be close to the south end of the air base. His stamina was weakened, his body was torn and beaten, and all that he had been through began taking its toll on him. He desperately needed to move on but his body was not cooperating. He was bogged down in the elephant grass. Just then he heard a voice and the last few words were: "Ain't no fucking way I'm abandoning you Rich and if any of you black pajama mother fuckers want to stop me come and get it!"

Risner smiled, recognizing the voice. "Dick, stay where you are I'm coming to you. Keep yelling so I'll know where you are." There was no response. "Dick where are you?" Again there was no response. With all the energy he had remaining, Major Risner ran as fast he could to where he had last heard Petterson's voice. He almost stumbled over him before he saw him. Petterson's eyes were closed and he was delirious, his foot and leg paralyzed by the snake venom. Risner cradled Petterson's head in his arm. "Dick, what is it, are you wounded?" Petterson got out the words snake and foot and Risner saw what he was talking about. "Dick, can you walk?" Risner asked.

"Must find the Major, I need to go" he muttered incoherently.

"Dick it's me, Rich, I've got to get you to a doctor," Risner answered.

Petterson opened his eyes and focused on Risner's face. "What took you so long? How was R & R?" he said weakly and then passed out.

Already past the point of exhaustion himself,

Major Risner picked Petterson up in the fireman's carry and he began to move in the direction he thought would take him to Highway 1, the highway between Da Nang and Saigon. He heard more aircraft overhead and figured he must be getting closer. He covered over 3 kilometers and was bone tired and weary. He had to put Petterson down for a minute while he regained his breath and strength. Petterson was unconscious. Risner checked his pulse. It was weak, but he was still alive.

While looking in the direction he thought he needed to go, he noticed dust in the distance and knew it must be Highway 1. He continued to follow the stream, as it got shallower until there was almost no water left in the stream. He left the streambed and with Petterson on his back, started running in the direction of Highway 1. He was 600 meters away. He crossed railroad tracks, came upon the highway, turned left and started running again. He continued to run with Petterson over his shoulder even as a couple of Vietnamese busses were passing him and looking at him in fascination. He kept running until he could run no farther and stopped in the middle of the road. He bent over to allow Petterson to lie down and he tried to catch his breath. As he rose he saw a figure a couple of clicks away waving at him and he waved back. He couldn't go any farther and he sat down in the middle of the road.

Within a couple of minutes, an Americal Division MP and jeep was at his side.

MP: "You wouldn't happen to be Major Risner, would you sir?"

Major Risner: "Yes, I would"

"Who is that lying on the ground?"

"My best friend."

MP: "Well, praise the Lord"

Risner: "You can say that again."

The MP saluted and said, "Welcome back, Major."

Major Risner: "It's good to be back. Take us home, please"

MP: "You've got it sir. It would be an honor".

HOMECOMING

Earlier that same morning, Major Tom Durham, a close friend of Major Risner's, came into the MAG-12 Civic Action Team's office with a couple of cardboard boxes and very somberly went to Risner's desk and started packing the contents of his desk. He never said a word, nor did any one in the office, as all knew what he was doing. Staff Sergeant Cong, Corporal McKillips and Corporal Hays watched.

Hays broke the silence, "What happens now?"

Durham replied, "After we finish making an inventory of Major Risner's personal effects, an official message will be sent to Headquarters Marine Corps in Washington, D.C., listing Major Risner as missing in action. A Marine Officer and a Navy Chaplain will then deliver a formal letter in person to Major Risner's family."

Hays couldn't hold back the tears and left the office area and went to his living quarters. The previous two nights he had remained at the rendezvous point through the evening and early morning hours, hoping and praying that Risner and Petterson would both be there. He hadn't slept since dropping off Petterson. After Durham left, Hays returned to the office area and his desk.

"I should have never let him go off alone," he said to no one in particular. McKillips responded, "How could you or anyone know?"

As the noon hour approached, the phone rang

and Hays answered it.

"Corporal Hays speaking sir. Say that again. You saw what?" He was getting excited.

"Where do you think you saw him?"

"Was anyone else with him? We'll be right there!" Hays let out a whoop for joy. "He's been spotted about 4 clicks south of the south gate and the Gunny is with him!" He exclaimed to Cong and McKillips.

The south gate was rarely used except by heavy equipment like earthmovers, etc.

"Grab your gear," he cried, "Let's go!" The three rushed to get their weapons and had just arrived at their vehicles when an Americal Division MP jeep pulled up with Major Risner. When Major Risner got out of the jeep everyone was whooping and cheering. His appearance spoke to the ordeal he had been through. He had no hat or shirt and his trousers were cutoff below the knees and his web belt was missing. He was wearing his boots without socks or shoelaces. His chest, back, arms and legs were covered with big red welts. He had rings around his eyes and his face and the top of his head was covered with scratches. His wrists looked like they had been rubbed raw almost to the bone. He had bruises all over.

The cheering stopped when everyone realized that Gunnery Sergeant Petterson was not with him. Reading everyone's thoughts, Risner explained: "Gunnery Sergeant Petterson is going to be alright. We met up and he was suffering from a snake bite. We dropped him off at the 2nd Surgical Hospital and after a preliminary examination, the doctor administered anti-venom. They think he will be alright because he didn't get enough venom to kill or paralyze him." Smiling, Risner said, "I will bet though the snake died from biting the Gunny." Everyone laughed.

Solemnly Risner said: "He rescued me. I owe him my life."

With that, he shook everyone's hand including the Group Commanding Officer and Executive Officer and all the other staff officers and enlisted who rushed out of their offices to see what was going on. Major Risner was surrounded by a group of over 30 people.

"It sure is good to see all of you."

The Group XO took over and drove Major Risner to the MAG-12 Dispensary for medical attention. Risner refused to go to the Army hospital.

"After they all get a load of Dick Petterson, they won't admit any more Marines," he quipped. Seriously he said, "I wouldn't have dropped him off there if I thought our Dispensary could take care of him. As for me, I'd rather have our Flight Surgeon take care of me."

Immediately after Risner left, Hays got on the phone with the 2nd Surgical Army hospital. One of the nurses tending to Petterson said that he was already coming around though still suffering from dehydration and the after-effects of the snake bite as well as the anti-venom. Waiting a couple of hours, Hays called sickbay and talked to the doctor who treated Major Risner. He told Hays that the Major had been severely beaten and prodded all over his body with bamboo sticks and rods. His toes were broken and his feet were swollen and he was severely bruised in the shoulder areas from his arms being dislocated several times. He was suffering from dehydration and malnutrition. The doctor said that he was allowing our S-2 to debrief him for a short time and then he told the Major that he was going to admit him as an inpatient. The doctor said that the Major politely declined his invitation to stay in the dispensary as he was going to go back to his quarters. The doctor said that he agreed only if Major Risner would take a shot (sedative). Major Risner agreed and the doctor told Hays because of the Major's size and condition, he gave him a triple dose of sedative to make sure he slept. The Group XO escorted the Major back to his quarters.

The same afternoon, the S-2 Officer, Captain Julius Jones came to the Civic Action Team office shortly after his first debriefing of Risner. Jones was visibly impressed by what he learned. "From the description he gave us, we have an idea where that NVA POW camp is in Laos. I have sent communications messages to 1st Wing and 1st Division as well as a personal message by courier to General Walt's office in Da Nang. General Walt has been calling me everyday since Risner was reported missing. What I can tell you of what I said to the General is that Risner used his training, his instinct and his never give up attitude to make his escape. He had the wherewithal to know when his enemy was most vulnerable; Major Risner beat the odds and become one of the few who successfully escaped. Not only did he escape, but he managed to link-up with Gunnery Sergeant Petterson.

175

According to Risner, Petterson showed up at just the right time when the Major could go no farther. Even though he was suffering from a snake bite, he guided the Major back to the MSR where they were spotted by one of the Americal Division MPs. Major Risner said that Gunnery Sergeant Petterson became unconscious by the time the MP showed up. I've got to tell you men, this is one remarkable story of two remarkable Marines!"

THE CELEBRATION

That night the MAG-12 Civic Action Team had a mini celebration. They had already decided to have the main celebration when Major Risner and Gunnery Sergeant Petterson were both well. Present were Captain Greenwold, Corporal Hays, Corporal McKillips and Private First Class Garry Williams as well as one of Petterson's friends, Staff Sergeant Clark. The Team had just brought out the wine when Charley decided to join the celebration. After the first rocket landed with that distinctive "crack!" everyone went outside to the bunker until it was safe to come out. Hays remarked to Staff Sergeant Clark, "That landed close."

Not hearing anything for another minute or so, Hays and Clark looked over the top and saw two red streaks leaving the tubes far away followed by the usual "thump!" sound. Clark grabbed Hays' jacket as he was going down and both heard loud cracks again. They looked up in time to see the dust and sand settling about 50 meters in front of them. "That was too damn close!" Clark exclaimed. "Come on Gene, if they're walking them in we don't need to stay here. Let's get to the command bunker".

Staff Sergeant Clark was Petterson's back-up in the command bunker. Off they went when another rocket landed about the same place as the other two. Another went off by the time they made it to the command bunker. The sirens were still going and everyone was assuming their defensive positions. Hays was on the radio talking to one of the tower spotters when to everyone's surprise, Major Risner walked in followed by Gunnery Sergeant Petterson and promptly asked "What's the situation Staff Sergeant Clark?" A cheer went up around the room. Hays said to no one in particular, "This man never fails to amaze me."

After all the welcome backs were given, Clark brought him up-to-date on the situation. The rockets had stopped, but a call came from the Group Guard on the southern perimeter that trip flares had gone off in the wire but the Marines were blinded by their own perimeter lights that were supposed to be cut-off whenever the base was under attack. This was a repeat of what happened during the TET Offensive. It not only blinded the Marines, but the lights exposed their positions. Major Risner quickly got on the phone to Chu Lai Defense Command and was talking to the new CLDC Commander, another Army Lieutenant Colonel. Risner explained the situation in explicitly terse language. Apparently the Colonel didn't appreciate this junior officer's attitude and said so. Major Risner's next statement was something to the effect that if he (the Colonel) didn't cut the lights immediately, Major Risner himself would come to CLDC and put out those lights along with the Colonel's running lights. The lights were extinguished soon after. Everyone would have cheered again, but no one dared, as they knew Major Risner was serious. Afterwards, he did have a grin on his face as did everyone else.

Several thoughts raced through Hays' mind:

pride of being a part of a remarkable group of men, thankfulness for the safe return of Risner and Petterson and the closeness and brotherhood of men in combat. Major Risner had brought himself home! It was remarkable. From approximately 35 kilometers away, he managed to orient himself with nothing but the stars at night, the sun during the day, coming within 6 kilometers of the base. He used surrounding vegetation for concealment and for nourishment. He paced himself, always keeping his eyes alert for danger. He pushed his body beyond the normal limits of endurance and willed himself to succeed. Many thoughts must have run through his mind but his one main objective was to get back to his unit and his men no matter what it took. His stamina, determination to survive and his love of family and Corps would not allow him to fail. Looking at the two men standing before him, Hays realized the bond between Risner and Petterson as well as their bond with the rest of the Team members was sealed forever.

The next day about 0800 Major Risner returned to his office. Everyone was concerned about him assuming his duties again so rapidly. No one at the Group Headquarters was going to question his decision and neither would anyone else. Risner called the XO and from the part of the conversation heard in the office, they had a mild disagreement about what would happen next. MAG-12 Intelligence as well as Americal Division Intelligence wanted to further debrief him immediately. Also, reports were required to all the command levels above, up to and including

Headquarters, United States Marine Corps. Added to that, the <u>Stars and Stripes</u> newspaper for the military had already caught wind of the story, and they wanted details. Much to the displeasure of many, Major Risner told the Group XO that not only would he not be meeting with any newspaper people, if they (the news reporters) wrote anything about his ordeal, they would become the next casualties of war. He also said that he needed to do one more thing before he would subjugate himself to any more debriefings or medical checks.

Whatever was said on the other end, Major Risner replied "Thank you, sir, I appreciate it," and he hung up the phone. Looking at Gunny Petterson and the Team, he smiled and asked: "What are all of you looking at? Grab your gear, Marines, we're going to town!"

The Team loaded up the same as they did on every other mission and everyone piled into the Cerlist with Major Risner riding in the back of the open area of the truck and they went right back to the place where Risner had been captured.

CONCLUSION

As the MAG-12 Civic Action Team left the main gate, some of the villagers in An Tan and other areas along the way actually came to the side of the road and waived at Major Risner. This was not the Vietnamese way. As the Team arrived at the departure point to Khuong Quang village, Major Risner saw a handful of villagers who were standing about 50 meters away. He waived at them and some waved back.

From amongst them, a young girl carrying a water lily came up to him and presented it arms outstretched. As he bent over to receive it, she had tears in her eyes as she said, "Ever since they take you, I wait for you to come back here at my Grandmother's house. This is for you Thieu Ta", and then, "I am so sorry". At this, Major Risner embraced her and whispered something in her ear. He hugged her again and over his shoulder told the Team that this was the girl, Phan Thi Lan, who had asked for his help when he had been captured.

As the young girl returned to the group, Major Risner waved at the villagers and everyone returned to their vehicles and the base. Major Risner reluctantly went back to Group Headquarters to be examined and debriefed again.

The next few days the Team didn't see much of him as everyone at Chu Lai in a position of authority wanted to talk to him. The same was true of Da Nang. Stories abounded around the base of his courage and physical stamina. Local Vietnamese leaders came to pay their respects and praise him. With less than a couple of weeks to rotate, the Marine Corps decided to bring him home right away. Captain Greenwold from 533 assumed the position of Civic Action Officer. Americal Division resumed control of Chu Lai Defense Command Sub-Sector Four. The Team had a hurried going away party for Major Risner but never got a chance to spend any more time with him. Dick Petterson helped him pack and saw him off. It was never the same again; the magic or "mojo" was not there.

EPILOGUE

This book is based on actual events in the lives of Major Richard F. Risner, First Sergeant Richard M. Petterson, and Master Sergeant Ronald E. Hays; all retired from the United States Marine Corps. Any errors, omissions or mischaracterizations are the sole fault of the author. Some of the names of characters in this book have been changed.

The success that the Marine Corps had with the Combined Action Platoons in Vietnam led to the creation of a secondary Military Occupational Specialty (MOS) designation of 8441, Civil Affairs NCO. A correspondence course was created by the Marine Corps Institute (MCI). Requirements for the MOS included completion of the course and minimum of 6 months on-the-job training in Vietnam. I was one of the first to complete the course and receive the MOS. After the Vietnam War ended, the Marine Corps retired the MOS, with the option to re-activate it in time of war. This is exactly what happened when the Afghanistan and Iraq Wars began. Civic Action groups were created with the same mission we had in Vietnam.

The Marine Corps Small Wars Manual of 1940, along with the personal Banana Wars experience of General Krulak was instrumental to the philosophy of Civic Action. This philosophy seems common sense in today's world, in that no matter where one travels or lives, knowledge and use of local language and customs engenders trust and friendship with indigenous people.

By reciprocating, teaching defensive tactics, use of weapons and by educating the general population in the principles of freedom and democracy, we build solid partners and friends. This is true nation building. My fellow Marines today carry on that proud tradition of an elite fighting force feared by our enemies while being welcomed as good neighbors and ambassadors for freedom by our friends.

Tsien Hsue-Shen was a real person and his story has been accurately told in this book. He was returned to China in September of 1955 after being under house arrest for almost 5 years. It was determined at the time that his return would not compromise our technology since he had been absent from working in his field for a sufficient period of time. Upon his return to China he did continue his rocket research. By 1960, Tsien launched the first Chinese-built R-2 Rocket. By 1970, he launched China's first satellite using his DF-2 rocket. In 1968 Tsien founded the Space Flight Medical Research Center to prepare for manned flights. The large two staged FB-1 and CZ-2 rockets, the basis for China's ICBM and all existing Chinese space launch vehicles, first flew in 1972. Launches of the FSW photo reconnaissance satellite, with a recoverable re-entry capsule nearly large enough to accommodate a pilot, began in 1974.

Tsien's manned spacecraft design proposed in the late 1970s was a winged spaceplane, launched by a CZ-2 core booster with two large strap-on boosters. It so strongly resembled the canceled US Dynasoar of 15 years earlier that US intelligence analysts wondered if it wasn't based on declassified Dynasoar technical information. It seems that this was to be preceded by a simpler manned capsule. First public announcement of the manned program came in February, 1978. By November the head of the Chinese Space Agency, Jen Hsin-Min, confirmed that China was working on a manned space capsule and a "Skylab" space station. In January, 1980 the Chinese press reported a visit with the Chinese astronaut trainees at the Chinese manned spaceflight training center. Photographs appeared of the astronauts in training. Pressure suited astronauts were shown in pressure chamber tests. Other trainees were shown at the controls of a space shuttle-like spaceplane cockpit. A fleet of ships for recovery of manned capsules at sea was built and in May of 1980, the first capsule was recovered from the South Pacific after a suborbital launch. However, suddenly in December of 1980, Wang Zhuanshan, the Secretary General of the New China Space Research Society and Chief Engineer of the Space Center of the Chinese Academy of Sciences, announced that Chinese manned flight was being postponed because of its cost. Fundamental economic development was given priority.

This was apparently Tsien's last attempt at a manned program while still actively heading the space program. Tsien managed to keep in the favor of the changing Chinese regimes over the years. He was a dedicated Communist whose technical advice on agriculture contributed to the death of millions during the Great Leap Forward in 1958. He met Mao six times and tutored him in 1964. He survived the Cultural

Revolution of 1968 and supported the Tienamen Massacre in 1989. His active career ended when he was awarded the State's highest award, State Scientist of Outstanding Contribution in October 1991. A new manned space program would be approved in 1992, led by leaders and engineers trained in Russia in the late 1950s. Tsien lived out the balance of his life in seclusion in a guarded residential compound in Beijing.

Richard F. Risner went on to make training films for the Marine Corps on escape and evasion. He spent many of those later years speaking at public engagements always downplaying his own heroics. Major Risner attended the first Prisoner of War Reunion hosted by President Nixon in Washington, D.C. He later told me that one of the former POW's (I'll call him Smith) came up to him, told him his name, and asked for the Major's name. When Major Risner gave his name, Smith said, "So you're the one!" Major Risner asked him what he meant by that. Smith asked him to wait a minute while he got some of his buddies before he explained. He returned with a small group of former POWs. Smith told the group, "This is Major Risner, the one who killed Honcho!" They all shook his hand and thanked him. They went on to explain that Honcho was one of the NVA leaders in charge of the POW camp where they were held and where Major Risner was being taken to before his escape. Honcho had delighted in torturing and abusing the prisoners. He was the most hated by all the POW's. Honcho, they further explained, was the one who brought in new prisoners to the compound. The prisoners heard that a

Marine Major had been captured and knew that Honcho was sent to escort him to the POW camp. When the VC returned to the compound, minus Honcho, they heard the story of how the Major had killed Honcho. Upon hearing this, the group of POW's came to attention, offered a salute to the Major and then began to sing "God Bless America." This so infuriated their captors, that the prisoners were tortured daily for the next 2 weeks. Upon hearing this, Major Risner broke down in tears and apologized for causing them hardship. Smith and the others quickly told Major Risner that it had been worth it to pay tribute to someone who had killed their worst enemy and one who had been the source of so much pain and agony inflicted on all the POW's.

After leaving Vietnam, I returned to Marine Corps Air Station, El Toro, California. I tried to re-enlist to go back to language school and become an interrogator translator, however the Marine Corps spent a lot of money on my training and my Avionics MOS was critically short-manned, so my request was denied. Instead, I opted to return to Memphis for advanced training of 32 weeks. Upon completion in 1969, I was selected to be an instructor at the basic and advanced Avionics schools. This ensured that I would remain in Memphis for another 3 years, otherwise I probably would have returned to Vietnam for a second tour. Major Risner and I kept in touch for a while and then lost touch. I was in the last few months of an advanced avionics course at Memphis in 1970, when I got word that he had been transferred to Memphis for duty. I could not believe my luck at getting to see him again. He was assigned duties as the Training Officer for Marine Aviation Training Support Group 90. Upon graduation from the advanced course and Instructor Basic Course, Major Risner, who was also acting XO for a time, arranged for me to be assigned to him for a period of 30 days before I began teaching. He was in the process of implementing an idea for a display for the public and some other government dignitaries including the Commandant of the Marine Corps and the Secretary of the Navy. His idea was to simulate an air and ground assault on a fortified enemy position. I did all the coordination between units and individuals and I was his assistant. I arranged with the Marine Air Reserve Squadron Commander, Major Tom Durham, for a simulated air strike using Marine A-4's. Major Durham was a decorated pilot from Vietnam and a personal friend of Major Risner's and mine from Vietnam. He was the officer who came to gather all of Rich's personal effects when we thought Rich was missing or captured. Major Durham was going to lead his A-4 and another for the simulated air strike. The other pilot during practice was reluctant to get too low, but Major Durham almost touched the bottom of his aircraft on the NVA flag atop the fortified position.

I also arranged for the Navy Search and Rescue Helicopter, an UH-34 used in Vietnam, to pick up the infantry platoon and drop them into their assault positions in order to attack the enemy bunker. All of the members of the infantry platoon were decorated veterans of the Vietnam War. Some of these Marines were recipients of the Bronze Star and Silver Star for heroism and gallantry against enemy forces and some were wounded in action, recipients of the Purple Heart. During practice and during the real performance, I was in the tower on the radio and PA system, calling in the air strike. Our ordnance personnel planted charges set off remotely as the A-4's led by Major Durham began their strafing attack. All of the ammunition and ordnance were flash and bang devices that gave the same effect of live ordnance. The Secretary of the Navy was not able to be there, but General Cushman, the Commandant of the Marine Corps was present and I was honored to meet him. The <u>Memphis Commercial Appeal</u> newspaper covered the event, as did one of the television stations. It was hailed by all as a huge success.

Not long after I began teaching, Major Risner was asked to speak at one of our monthly 56 club luncheons. The 56 club was an enlisted club for all E-5's and E-6's both Navy and Marines. Previous guests included the Mayor of Memphis, the Honorable Henry Loeb, who had been a' PT boat commander during World War II and had served with former President John Kennedy. Another was the "Galloping Ghost", Red Grange, former NFL great and member of the Hall of Fame. There were typically 100 or more in attendance at one of these luncheons. Major Risner asked that I be there in the audience. As a result of the word being spread around the base of his upcoming speaking engagement, there were over 200 sailors and Marines in attendance. After he was introduced, he began to tell his audience of what he did in Vietnam. He talked a lot about the Civic Action Team and then told his audience about his capture and subsequent escape without going into details. After speaking for about 45 minutes, he said that he would take questions. I rose and without introducing myself, asked him if he would tell us more about his escape. He smiled and began by saying that when he was first captured he wished that Sergeant Hays (me) had been able to come to his aid. He then explained our relationship in combat. Now all eyes were on me! I really didn't expect that, but then the Major always did the unexpected.

As Major Risner always liked to do things in a big way, he organized the annual Marine Corps Golf Tournament of 1970 at Millington. There has never been another like it before or since. For a ridiculous entry fee of $5 per golfer ($10 per team) we got 36 holes of golf, 18 on Saturday and 18 on Sunday and that included green fees and cart rentals. Included was a steak dinner following Sunday's round with an awards ceremony and free drinks. Top prizes included sets of golf clubs and bags. To top it off, we had Women Marines dressed in yellow silk shirts and red hot pants delivering beer from electric golf carts on the course for $.50 a beer! All you had to do was raise your hand and they came to you. Saturday's round started at 0800 and didn't finish until 2 hours after dark as a result. It was decided that beer would not be served on the course during Sunday's round of golf. After everyone finished their golf rounds on Sunday, we gathered at the lake house on base for the banquet and awards ceremony. It was fantastic.

In 1973, only 2 years after the birth of our second son, Eric, I was transferred overseas again to the First Marine Aircraft Wing in Iwakuni Japan. After arriving there, I found my old unit MAG-12 from Vietnam and was initially assigned to them. I was reassigned from there to MAG-15, part of Task Force Delta in Nam Phong, Thailand. MAG-15 had been in Thailand for over 12 months during the last combat phases of the Vietnam War. Aircraft from MAG-15 were bombing in South Vietnam to provide close air support for the ARVNs as well as missions assigned in Laos and Cambodia.

When President Nixon ordered the bombing halt as a result of the peace negotiations with North Vietnam, I accompanied the VMFA-232 Red Devils to Cubi Point in the Philippines for 3 months and then returned to Iwakuni. MAG-15 was the last official combat unit in the Vietnam War.

Returning home in 1974, I was assigned as an instructor to the CH-53 Sikorsky Sea Stallion Trainer at Marine Corps Helicopter Station, Tustin California. During the four years I spent there, I was in contact with both Rich Risner and Dick Petterson. Rich received a medical retirement at Camp Pendleton and Dick retired as a First Sergeant at El Toro. During those years both of them were frequent guest speakers, telling our Vietnam story. After the fall of Saigon and evacuation of remaining American personnel and Vietnamese, a small tent city was set-up at Camp

Pendleton for the first refugees. I volunteered to assist in this effort as they were looking for Marines trained in the Vietnamese language, but the Marine Corps would not allow me to go as I was needed as an Instructor at the CH-53 trainer. Major Risner and 1st Sergeant Petterson spent many days going through the refugee village trying to find Staff Sergeant Cong, the Khoi family or anyone we knew from Chu Lai, with negative results. We all heard first hand information from the refugees that after the fall of Saigon, many of the ARVN Officers were summarily executed as well as any military, civilian or political people who aided American Armed Forces. All of the surviving ARVN soldiers were placed in re-education camps for periods of 3-5 years and they were required to take an oath of allegiance to the new government.

In 1978, I was selected to serve as an Assistant Aviation Monitor at Headquarters Marine Corps in Washington D.C., actually located at the Navy Annex in Arlington. I was in charge of the assignments and classifications of over 7000 enlisted Marines stationed throughout the World. I did pre-screening for all of the maintenance personnel assigned to the Presidential Helicopter Squadron based at Quantico and screening for all of the Marine aviation instructors throughout the Naval Air Maintenance Training Group.

In 1981, I was assigned to the Naval Air Station at Memphis and assisted in the creation and implementation of the Enlisted Aviation Maintenance Trainee Management Unit. We were responsible for ensuring the follow on-training and permanent assignment of all Marine enlisted aviation trainees upon the completion of their basic aviation skills training. I was later promoted to Master Sergeant and became the Assistant Director of Training until my retirement in 1986. During these years I remained in touch with both Rich and Dick.

Dick Petterson went back to school after retirement and graduated with a Bachelor of Arts Degree in English from Cal State, San Bernardino. He opened his own business at Big Bear Lake and 25 years later sold it and moved near the Marine Corps Mountain Warfare School in northern California. His wife Margo is a successful artist and has won several competitions. You can see her website at: http://www. margopetterson.com, "The Feminine West" and I think her paintings to be some of the most realistic and beautiful I have ever seen. Their daughter Sandra is a Seabee and a veteran of the Iraq War. I try to keep in constant touch with Dick. I am always renewed in spirit when I talk to him and together we strive to keep our story alive.

Rich Risner became friends with a Hollywood stuntman and was in a few movies. He was a stuntman in The Great Waldo Pepper and was an extra in The Stuntman. His health began to further deteriorate and he had open heart surgery. During this time, he stayed with Dick for a while and Dick helped him get back into shape. While he temporarily regained his physical health, he was having to deal with problems from two previous marriages and was still haunted from the memory of the black ops mission and his Vietnam experience as a POW. Dick credits his 3rd wife Lynda with turning Rich's life around and providing him with love and support that continued up until his last moments. Lynda told me that the physical toll of his military service and occasional bad dreams and night sweats were wearing on him until the end.

Only a few months before his death, Rich Risner shared his story with me about the events that took place in South Korea as well as details concerning his torture and abuse by his NVA captors. The last time I was able to speak to him before he went into the hospital he gave me permission to write his story. He lived with the guilt since that operation until his death. The source of that guilt was the after-knowledge that he had been selected for this assignment because he knew the "John" that was killed. He had gone to high school with "John" and knew his parents but had lost track of him as he went off to college. It was not revealed to Rich that John was the person they were looking for until right before the operation. He was completely surprised and looked forward to rescuing his friend from school. What Rich didn't know, but his CIA handler knew, was that John had defected and they (CIA) knew he would not voluntarily return with the two Marines; in other words, it was a hit job.

On January 27th of 2005, with his family present, Rich Risner was transferred to the Kingdom of Heaven. Lynda told me that Rich actually passed with a smile on his face. His health had deteriorated to the point that he was glad to get some relief. He wanted to live but not be seen in the condition he was in at the time he died. Rich was buried with full military honors at the National Veteran's Cemetery in Riverside, California. Lynda told me that he knew how much we all loved him and respected him. I always treasured the time we had together.

1996 was a year of tragedy and adventure for me. I lost my youngest brother Chris, when he was only 42 years old due to a massive heart attack. Chris gave me the encouragement and support to begin writing about my Vietnam experience. I had just interviewed and was selected for a job overseas when Chris died. His death devastated my Mom and Dad and Brother Russ and me and Chris's lovely wife Nancy and three beautiful daughters. After the memorial service, I came home briefly and then went to my new job assignment in Jeddah, Kingdom of Saudi Arabia. My title was Senior Consultant to the Royal Saudi Naval Forces. I trained their naval enlisted personnel in basic skills and basic electronics in preparation for attending our naval aviation schools in Pensacola Florida. After less than a year, the Saudis cancelled our contract citing the cost of the Gulf War and other reasons. After that, I taught electronics at a small 2 year college, worked in the banking industry and now I work part-time as a Customer Service Manager for Wal-Mart in Oxford, Mississippi. My wife Barbara and her parents and siblings are all from the Oxford area. She works at the Oxford Eagle newspaper.

My father served in the Marine Corps during World War II and I am very proud of my son Eric now serving in Iraq. He has served previous tours of duty in

Afghanistan and South Korea. My other two sons are both professional drivers. As for me, I try to spend more time with my wife Barbara and our five grandchildren and tell our story to as many people as I can about all of those who served so honorably during the Vietnam War and many of whom have suffered terribly as a result. I salute them and say, "Welcome home brothers, welcome home."

Gene Hays
Oxford, MS
April 12, 2010

PS: Special thanks to my Mom and Barbara for their proof reading and a special thanks to Jon Scott for his constructive criticism.

7066828R0

Made in the USA
Lexington, KY
16 October 2010